IS THE CHURCH ARMED BUT NOT DANGEROUS?

HOW HIS BELOVED BRIDE BECOMES A BATTLE-READY WARRIOR THROUGH SIX PRAYER PRINCIPLES

JEFF BUTLER

ENDORSED BY TOMMY TENNEY

ARMED BUT NOT DANGEROUS

Copyright © 2006 Jeff Butler

ISBN-13: 978-1-886296-41-1
ISBN-10: 1-886296-41-3

Printed in the United States of America
All rights reserved

All Scripture quotations, unless otherwise noted, are taken from the New King James Version (NKJV). Copyright © 1982 by Thomas Nelson, Inc. Used by permission. All rights reserved.

Arrow Publications
P.O. Box 10102
Cedar Rapids, IA 52410
Phone: (319) 395-7833
Toll Free: (877) 363-6889 (U.S. only)
Fax: (319) 395-7353
Web: www.arrowbookstore.com

Dedication

Long before we began pastoring in Racine, Wisconsin, the intercessors at True Life Ministries were praying. God only knows how much more these dedicated people of prayer could have accomplished if they had the teaching, understanding and inspiration of the modern, organized prayer movement.

It was an easy decision to dedicate this book on prayer to the prayers, both original and recent, who continue to surround Tami, myself, our children and the church with constant, loyal, powerful prayer. We could not be more blessed; they could not be more anointed or appointed.

Intercessors, this dedication from me seems small compared to your dedication to Him. You literally moved many of us from *armed but not dangerous* to *armed and dangerous* to the devil. Thanks for your unselfish commitment to establish and expand the kingdom of God. You are the best on the planet.

Contents

Prologue
 Introduction

1. A Cosmic Conflict 15
2. Protected But Not Productive 35
3. Protected But Not Passionate 53
4. Prepared But Not Progressing 71
5. Persuasion Brings Protection 89
6. Protected and Profound 107
7. Success with a Sword 121
8. Walk the Warrior's Talk 137

Epilogue

Endorsements

I have known Jeff Butler for many years. I have witnessed him transition as he moved from the physical activity of athletics into the spiritual authority of prayer by using the principles outlined here. He now shows how to successfully battle in the heavenly realm. In his new book, *Armed But Not Dangerous,* he takes us from playing soldier to being soldiers. You need to read this book.

P.S. The bride wears combat boots!

Tommy Tenney
God Chasers Network, Pineville, LA

Jeff Butler has presented a powerful position of TRUTH in this book. *Armed But Not Dangerous* provides us with a true glimpse into realities of the Western church today. The warfare necessary to displace and replace demonic rule must be undertaken by the believers who are ARMED and willing to engage. Jeff's inspirational style and motivational focus offer the reader practical steps for involvement, and provide tools every believer can use as they become engaged in this effort. Globally, spiritual warfare is going to another level, and this book will serve you well in your quest to bring down Satan's kingdom.

Very well written!

Bishop Tudor Bismark
Jabula—New Life Ministries, Harare, Zimbabwe

I recently finished a series of messages for our church on spiritual warfare and the armor of God. Our congregation is fairly mature in their understanding of the Word. However, these messages seemed to be particularly timely as our people drank in the reality of our times.

Pastor Jeff Butler is a seasoned pastor/teacher with many years of experience in the ministry. This book will place a manual for victory in the hands of every hungry and searching person. Pastor Butler's experience as a pastor, regularly involved in the day-to-day lives of Christians, will provide practical insights that will set people free to serve the kingdom with intelligence and discernment.

BISHOP JOSEPH L. GARLINGTON, SR, PHD
Covenant Church of Pittsburgh and Reconciliation Ministries Int'l

In this day of spiritual drought, the world awaits a fresh breeze and gentle rain from our Lord. Jeff Butler's handling of this anointed word on prayer and spiritual warfare refreshes the thirsty and parched soul. Read it and receive a deeper meaning of the warring bride in intimate discourse with her Lord.

BISHOP JACK DEHART
Chairman, Global Network of Christian Ministries, Dallas, TX

Prayer is the undisputed need of the church for every generation. It is the fuel that drives the engine. Jeff Butler has given us an excellent look at prayer. He shows us why we, at times, have been ineffective in our approach, and then gives the antidote for ineffective prayer. This book needs to be read by every person who is concerned about the direction of the church.

EDDIE CUPPLES
Love and Truth Ministries, Jackson, TN

Jeff Butler has given the church one of the best handbooks ever written on spiritual warfare! It is both biblically insightful and highly practical. Whoever reads it will come away being **truly armed and truly dangerous!**

DENNIS CRAMER
Dennis Cramer Ministries, South Williamsport, PA

Prologue

A Wife or a Warrior?

I married up . . . no doubt about it.

I shall never forget when she walked down the aisle to the front of the church that beautiful June day in 1981. Back then I thought she was everything I wanted a bride to look like; today I know she is everything I want a wife to be. I've made some boneheaded decisions down through the years, but my judgment in this case was right on. I knew what I wanted and went for it.

Men, if you are like I am, you chose your wife for the strength of her character, not her bench-pressing ability. We should be more impressed with quiet confidence and femininity than loud, overbearing brashness. The Scriptures clearly celebrate ladylike virtues in a woman, and I couldn't agree more. I like a lady to look and act ladylike. My bride, on that day, was just that . . . a picture-perfect bride.

I married a wife, not a warrior . . . a lover, not a fighter. Her training was not in the fine points of military maneuvers but in Christian character and godly virtues. She was dressed for a wedding, not a war. She was not weighed down with full military gear or battle fatigues, but wore a beautiful wedding gown. She knew where she was going and why she was going there; she dressed accordingly.

But the beauty of a bride on her wedding day cannot be sustained indefinitely. When a woman becomes a mother, an interesting transition takes place. When a mother's protective instincts kick in, her resolve and determination expand from that of being a wife for her husband to that of being a warrior over her children. God hardwired women to meet the demanding challenge of being a wife and mother. While I need my wife, our children need their mother to war for their welfare. What a daily balancing act it must require to be both.

THE OCCASION DETERMINES THE OUTFIT

Everyone has been invited to a party or function and not been clear on what you were expected to wear. "Should I wear a black tie and tails or blue jeans and boots?" can usually be answered by the nature of the event.

If the occasion determines the outfit, we should find out where we are headed . . . or better, we should find out who we are. Sometimes the bride should dress like a chaste virgin, awaiting her departure to the marriage celebration. But on other occasions the mother will look like a battle-ready warrior, desperately wanting dominion.

> I think we are preoccupied with our departure to a wedding in heaven, forgetting our responsibility to wage warfare for dominion on the earth.

If the bride is only prepared for a wedding she will be destroyed during the heat of a military campaign. On the other hand, a woman focusing only on waging war will not fulfill her role as a wife. How can one woman be pure as a virgin on her wedding day and powerful as a victorious warrior in the heat of battle?

Every woman must determine the occasion and put on the appropriate outfit; so should the church.

THE CHURCH IS A WOMAN WHO WARS

You and I represent the church, which is the bride of Christ. We are the bride; Jesus is the bridegroom. However, I think we are preoccupied with our departure to a wedding in heaven, forgetting our responsibility to wage warfare for dominion on the earth.

Being focused on exiting instead of overcoming has made us forget that what was "given by grace" must be gained by conquering. Sometimes we act like a confused wife, not a conquering warrior!

One retreat speaker tells us to rest in our inheritance as the Lord's bride, but the next revival speaker tells us to war for the same inheritance. Sounds confusing until you recall—inheritance is based on whose family you're in, not which enemy you fight. To get our inheritance of kingdom victory and authority, we must have faith in our Father's gifts, yet often we must fight. It takes both . . . faith and fight.

The Lord fell in love with His bride, the church, but kingdom expansion demands this lovely lady transition into a warrior. To only be His bride is to ignore the mandate to establish His kingdom by conquest. While we remain His wife, we must also become the warrior/mother who can advance the kingdom of God. God hardwired us to be both.

The question becomes: When should the church be a wife and when/how should the church be a warrior? The answer: Discern the occasion. Remember, occasion determines the outfit. We need discernment to appraise the occasion. We have the armor issued . . . we just need to know when to put it on and how to use it. Sometimes the occasion is a formal function calling for black tie and tails; other times the church should come dressed for battle. Often we are summoned in our spirit to be close to His heart, but more often we are sent into a kingdom conflict to establish His headship.

This book will answer how the Lord's beloved wife can also be a battle-ready warrior by activating six practical prayer principles. The wife can become a warrior! She will be armed and dangerous. It can only happen because of prayer.

Would you like to become dangerous to the devil—by defeating selfishness, self-righteousness, confusion, the opportunistic enemy, double-mindedness, and poor continuity?

By using the prayer principles listed at the end of each chapter, our "less than mediocre" can be turned into "more than a conqueror." We can attack back.

1. Prayer Principle of Maturity: Deals with Selfishness
2. Prayer Principle of Passion: Deals with Self-Righteousness
3. Prayer Principle of Right Timing: Deals with Confusion
4. Prayer Principle of Persuasion: Deals with the Opportunistic Enemy
5. Prayer Principle of Focus: Deals with Double-mindedness
6. Prayer Principle of Dividing and Discerning: Deals with Continuity

INTRODUCTION

Little Arlie looked silly . . . no, more than that, he looked ridiculous. It wasn't his fault. When he arrived at the service, he was appropriately dressed for the evening. However, by the time we finished "outfitting" him . . .

Let me explain. When I accepted the invitation to speak at a statewide evangelism conference for a major denomination, they assigned the following subject to me: "Armed and Dangerous."

This theme, supported by the Ephesians 6 description of a spiritual soldier, provided much preaching material and this vivid illustration . . . Arlie, dressed as a spiritual serviceman. When I finally finished equipping my little helper, he could barely move. My suit coat for a breastplate; a short blanket tucked into his belt representing the Girdle of Truth; a hat, reluctantly donated by a visiting minister for the Helmet of Salvation. He stood on cardboard to symbolize military footwear. He held a microphone stand—Sword of the Spirit—in one hand, and a cymbal—Shield of Faith—in the other.

When I realized he could hold or wear nothing more, I said, "Arlie may be armed but he certainly isn't dangerous, at least not to anybody but himself." I went on to say, "We have equipped him, but now he must activate this equipment. He isn't going to be a real offensive threat to any enemy when he can barely defend himself. *He is armed, but not dangerous.*"

"But there is one more thing Arlie can do; one way he still can fight," I said as I took his mouth and made it open and close like a puppet. "He can still use his mouth to shout for the victory, and he can still pray." Then I quoted verse 18 of Ephesians 6:

Praying always with all prayer and supplication in the Spirit, being watchful to this end with all perseverance and supplication for all the saints.

I believe Arlie, with full battle gear on, accurately describes our current spiritual state. We look the part, but the enemy doesn't judge us on looks. Looking dangerous is different than being dangerous. Prayer and praise used to activate spiritual armor transforms otherwise innocuous, banal Christians into active, operative soldiers.

I believe these specific prayer strategies will help us to launch a bold, new offensive against our enemy. It is time for the church to become aggressive again. I know this book will help.

— CHAPTER ONE —

A Cosmic Conflict

As humans, we inhabit a world originally used for Lucifer and his fallen angels. He was here first. The destination of the displaced rank and file of heaven, according to the Bible, was earth. With all of the possible places God could have chosen as a home for His creation called man, I wonder why He chose an environment already inhabited by those sent here as a punishment for pride and rebellion.

Why place delicate, innocent and fragile humans in this cosmic conflict zone where Lucifer has been placed on house arrest? The survival possibilities for God's physical creation seem significantly reduced when exposed to these spiritual entities of evil now inhabiting earth.

We have reason to believe that God was repentant that He placed man on the earth, quite possibly because of the dangerous exposure to a spiritual conflict between good and evil (see Genesis 6:6). Like Job, we have been enlisted in a spiritual conflict. We have not been punished, but promoted, by being cast into this cosmic crossfire. Job was offered to Satan when God asked, "Have you considered Job?" (Job 1:8) Man caught in God's battle . . . was this coincidence or divine strategy? If God strategically brought us into a pre-existing war, He will also equip us . . . He has equipped us for kingdom conflict.

Limited by Love

Some believe if God truly loved us, He would have left us out of His battle. I believe His divine love not only allowed but also encouraged our involvement in His war. God's love for us limited Him from getting involved in this cosmic conflict, much like a parent restricts their involvement by allowing the painful process of permitting children to learn, grow and mature through life's difficulties. The invaluable strength and insight gained through these struggles are the very things necessary to succeed in life and to establish His kingdom. Just like adult interference can prolong the development process in children, I think God steps back to encourage us to step up!

Someone recently told me of a friend of theirs who was training to work as a physical therapist to the handicapped. To better understand the challenges of his patients, although he was completely healthy, he lived as a quadriplegic for two weeks.

During this role-playing, he fell out of his chair one afternoon and laid on the floor of his home for 7–8 hours while he waited for help to arrive. Even with the phone a few feet away, he limited himself to the restrictions of a quadriplegic when faced with this physically painful and emotionally exhausting dilemma.

The physical pain came because of the fall to the floor and the emotional pain was the result of not knowing when, or if, help would arrive. He might be there 30 minutes, 3 hours or even longer, so physically he remained immobile while he mentally paced himself with patience. When asked why he didn't get up off the floor, "I couldn't" was his simple yet amazing reply.

Oh, he could have gotten up if he hadn't limited himself by love. He could have gotten up if he wasn't so committed and dedicated. He could have gotten up if he was defining himself by strength or ability. But because he was defining himself by love, he could not—would not—get up.

God is not incapable, in regard to His power, of taking us out of this cosmic conflict. But, because He is bound by His love for us, He can't remove us from the process needed for the development of spiritual skill necessary for kingdom conquest. Our involvement and exposure to this process promotes victory and allows spiritual success. This might help explain the seeming lack of concern God showed by putting us in this conflict.

To compensate for our apparent disadvantage and to assist us in this battle not of our choosing, God, because of love for us and belief in us, limited Himself to the incarnation so He could enter the human experience. God took on human form, that He might become a merciful high priest (see Hebrews 2:17), preparing us for battle.

The incarnation did not teach God what human pain and difficulty were, but it removed any doubt on our part that He understood our plight. This illustrates God's mercy and reveals the partnership and the co-laboring aspect of our great God.

Our spiritual leader does not operate as an aloof, distant commander secluded by thick-walled buildings or deep bunkers. He has not protected Himself, like some leaders, with layers of military manpower, but occupies the foxhole with each of us, wearing in His body the wounds of the conflict (just look in His hands, feet and side). He, fighting and co-laboring with us, has enlisted us to help Him win the war. This provides the best support possible for a battle that goes beyond physical engagement and includes the intangible (see Hebrews 11:1).

RIGHT WEAPON . . . WRONG TIME

Jesus exemplified the spiritual nature of the conflict during His arrest in the garden of Gethsemane. Impetuous Simon Peter, responding to a physical threat to Jesus, reacted with admirable loyalty by lopping off an ear of the high priest's soldier with his sword. However, Peter's weapon of choice would not work in the kingdom Jesus was entering. The response provided by Jesus clarifies the method required to accomplish victory in cosmic conflict (see Matthew 26:52–54).

Jesus told Simon Peter he would not win this conflict with conventional military means. He illustrated how spiritual understanding is necessary. The cutting off of Malchus' ear represented a false and temporary victory, which need not be celebrated. In essence, Jesus illustrated a new and innovative way of conducting war through the spiritual method made available because of Calvary. Peter mishandled the physical and missed this true spiritual concept.

Although Peter had been told by Jesus to take a sword for his journey, he did not have the wisdom to use it appropriately: right weapon—wrong time. Real spiritual battles cannot be fought on a physical plane by using admirable devotion yet questionable discretion.

> Real spiritual battles cannot be fought on a physical plane by using admirable devotion yet questionable discretion.

Things we think should qualify us as spiritual soldiers actually disqualify us. Instead of showing our maturity or spiritual sophistication by what we say, what we do or where we go (all physical expressions), some physical outbursts actually reveal our shortsightedness and shallowness. The fact that Jesus healed the servant's ear emphatically illustrates Peter's indiscretion.

When interrogated by Pilate (see John 18:36), Jesus answered by saying that if His kingdom were of this world His servants would fight. Jesus, in essence, told Pilate that the war was on a different plane and would be won by different means.

If Jesus' servants had employed physical intervention, they would have disqualified themselves from the very thing Jesus would use to save them . . . the cross. Man must not hinder but help accomplish God's redemptive work through the cross, for it will accomplish the ultimate defeat of the devil and secure victory for all mankind. We need to understand and appropriate the blood of Jesus afresh.

Battle Protection

Thankfully, we have not been ill-equipped for this cosmic conflict but have been given the wherewithal to establish His kingdom. Our king has not sent us into His battle without issuing appropriate armor. We have the armor of God! We have sufficient weaponry and have been thoroughly instructed in the elements of its use. The armor of God provides everything needed to prevail.

In Ephesians 6:12–17, we are briefed on our enemy and we receive our battle assignment. A vivid image of a soldier comes to mind when reading these verses. This is a soldier aptly armed—his hands are full, his body covered; he can hold or wear nothing more. Let's take a brief look at these provisions.

1. Waist Apron: To protect the reproductive areas
2. Breastplate: To protect the respiratory and circulatory systems
3. Footwear: To bruise the enemy's head with our heel
4. Shield: To forcefully knock down the opponent and to ward off incoming artillery
5. Headgear: To protect the body's master control center
6. Sword: To divide, destroy, and discern

Playing Not To Lose

How many times have we witnessed a basketball team go into a "stall" offense and eventually lose the game. A "stall" offense, where the ball is held so time can run off the clock when your team is ahead, often backfires. In football this is referred to as a "prevent defense." Theoretically, a prevent defense is designed to let the opponent gain yardage in small proportions rather than large amounts quickly. The team using this style of defensive wants the clock to run out before the big play gains yardage.

Our spiritual strategy should not be to prevent the devil from scoring more points before the game clock expires. Our focus should be on defeating the enemy—not just trying to prevent him from large gains. In this cosmic conflict, if we only try to survive until the clock expires and the King returns, we probably will lose.

I hear God calling us back to the offensive. He wants His team to advance and score so we can win the game, not just hang on hoping the devil doesn't score big. Jesus did not suffer and die just to tie the score . . . He wants us to win.

God did not send us into this game to play to a "draw" with the devil, but to be more than conquerors. The church must win . . . I know we will win! Winning is more than playing not to lose.

Once we have taken up this armor, we receive final instructions to "stand." This involves holding one's position and resisting—not retreating—from the enemy. Standing and not surrendering will help one prevail against the opposition, but our victory is not automatic just because we stand. We must not go into a stall offense.

The ultimate victory has already been secured through the blood of Jesus, but the responsibility of the spiritual soldier remains: we must preserve and maintain what has been won. Appropriating what has already been given is no easy assignment.

An Old Testament example comes to mind. Joshua, although given the land of Canaan through the promise of the Lord, had to fight for what had been given. Battles still had to be fought and blood shed to secure this new land. Joshua and his armies had to advance and win. It cost them to take what God had given, because it cost God to give it.

The city of Ai serves as an example (see Joshua 8). After a failed first attempt because of unconfessed sin, the second time God told

Joshua the city had been given unto him. Yet he and 30,000 of his soldiers planned and implemented an offensive thrust to take what God had given. In essence, what God gave them was the capability to conquer.

Sometimes people and armies play not to lose instead of playing to win, but conversely Joshua went after all that was possible. He did not stand still and wait on something or someone else. Often we equate standing our ground as the only significant accomplishment.

Spiritual success may begin with standing, but it must eventually include advance. Prayer makes standing against relentless assaults and advancing into the covenant promise much more possible.

> It cost them to take what God had given, because it cost God to give it. In essence, what God gave them was the capability to conquer.

Three general stages define our current approach to serving God: the negative (fallen down), the neutral (standing) and the positive (going). We cannot advance from a fallen position. In the natural, we are more excited when our children learn to walk than crawl. We teach our children to stand so they can walk. It would be very disconcerting if, after having learned to stand, our children don't walk or run. We seldom list how often our kids fall or celebrate their simply standing, but we get most excited when they first walk. There is just something about getting up and going.

The people of God must go deeper into the great commission, and because we cannot go from a fallen position, we must stand so we can go. There is a lot of work to be done . . . let's stand—let's go!

Listen to the instructions to stand found in verses 11–13 of Ephesians 6:

- **Stand** against the wiles (scheming plan) of the devil.
- That you may be able to **withstand** in the evil day.

- Having done all, to **stand**.
- **Stand** therefore.

It may appear that this soldier has only taken a defensive posture. However, "to stand" is an important military tactic. We need to remember that standing is not just the absence of falling—it provides the opportunity for advance. We need to be like our children; don't stand up just to stand . . . stand up to go!

Every Sunday, churches are filled with people who stand to sing, stand to worship, and stand to pray the benediction prayer. This should not reflect our biggest spiritual success of the week. We must remember: the Christian life is more than surviving from Sunday to Sunday. We must not only maintain but also prevail and advance.

The Whole Armor of God

The armor of God and battle instructions have been listed in Ephesians 6, but how can we adequately employ all God has given? Are there no additional military strategies to consider? If these six pieces represent all the equipment we need, and we have put them on, there should be guaranteed strength and power in the Lord (see Ephesians 6:10).

I see a lot of soldiers outfitted with the armor, but unfortunately few of them truly exert the power of God's might. Because of our survival mindset, we equate "standing" with having on complete military apparatus. Standing is not the end or the ultimate spiritual success.

If the only criteria we use for evaluating our armor and judging our spiritual success is *standing*, we may need to consider the context in its fullness. The power and might of the Lord must be used for more than "not failing or falling." There must be more to our spiritual success than just standing!

Too often the church resembles a boxer who tries to win a bout by only avoiding a knockout. We are in the ring, ducking and dodging the swings from our opponent, just hoping to be quick enough to get out of the way. At a certain point, the professional boxer must fight back if he expects to win . . . and so must the church. That's why it is not appropriate to only judge our spiritual success by the following two criteria:

> Too often the church resembles a boxer who tries to win a bout by only avoiding a knockout. At a certain point, the professional boxer must fight back if he expects to win.

1. Are we still standing? (Can we withstand the attack?)
2. Are we appointed with the correct armor? (Do we have all the protection possible?)

Although there are seasons when answering "yes" to these first two questions represents victory, I believe we must answer another important question:

3. Are we advancing the cause of the kingdom by defeating the devil?

The enemy of our spiritual progress takes delight in keeping us from advancing toward and establishing kingdom authority. There must be progress. There must be a time to advance and pursue, not just stand and defend.

The evil nature of our enemy explains why we need divine armor if we are to stand. According to apostle Paul, we are in a battle against a wicked adversary and this powerful opponent makes all available armor absolutely necessary if we are to survive and succeed in this cosmic conflict.

Our great Commander-in-Chief has not given us inadequate protection or instruction. We can move from the defensive to the offensive by operating with power and authority (see 2 Corinthians 10:4).

How can an inanimate object like spiritual armor have power? The Lord has given us the opportunity of prayer to help apply the armor and activate the soldier. Notice, Paul doesn't use an exclamation point or even a period, but a comma, as he continues on to the topic of prayer from the subject of the armor (see Ephesians 6:18).

> The problem is not the absence of armor but inadequate activation of the soldier wearing the armor.

This pointedly suggests that we cannot be finished until we have prayed. The problem is not the absence of armor but inadequate activation of the soldier wearing the armor. The real problem is that our armor is ineffective outside the context of prayer. Paul did not talk about the armor apart from the admonition to be always praying. Likewise, the effective soldier who heeds Paul's instruction must not engage the enemy without prayer.

We have been given the vital weapon of prayer. Properly applied, it helps make valuable and viable the armor already issued. Paul, speaking to the church of Corinth, spends many verses discussing God's involvement in his life. Then he turns to the church and says, *you helping together in prayer* (see 1 Corinthians 1:1–11). Helping God help the church can happen through prayer. We have a big God who allows us to participate in the process of activating the soldier and his armor.

The soldier and his armor may be capable enough, but prayer gives authority that helps prepare the spiritual soldier. Prayer makes the soldier even more effective.

Why would God enlist you and not commission you? Why would He empower you and not use you? Why equip and not direct? Why would God enable and not send us out through the power of prayer?

The devil willingly permits us to gather all the equipment we want, as long as we don't use it against him. Satan will not fight to take your ministry, your talents or gifts if you aren't using them. If we bury our talents because we don't want to lose them, the devil is delighted. He longs for the day when we return to our Master only what we had been given (see Matthew 25:14–30).

PERFECTION AND PRAYER

The Bible emphasizes being perfect. In almost every Bible reference, the words *perfect* and *complete* could be interchanged without any textual violation. In Ephesians, we find an admonition to "put on the whole armor of God." The soldier at that point would be perfect or complete. But many saints dressed for battle remain incomplete because of lack of prayer.

Have we fully comprehended how the power of prayer can help us launch a bold new offensive? Prayer makes us perfect or complete. Author Arthur Gordon said, "Once you have prayed you can do nothing more than pray, but until you have prayed you cannot do anything more than pray." Prayer brings completion and promotes full activation of the soldier and his armor. Completion or perfection outside of prayer as listed in Ephesians 6, for the spiritual soldier, is doubtful.

> If we bury our talents because we don't want to lose them, the devil is delighted.

TO WHOM DO THE GATES BELONG?

An ancient city serious about defending itself reinforced the protective wall and the gates to the city. For maximum security and protection, the walls must be constructed as impregnable as possible, yet allowing access through the gates. Regardless of how well one fortifies the wall, the gates remain the most vulnerable part of a city's plan of defense. In the absence of a good offense, the walls and gates become even more important as a defensive tool. In ancient times, the gates were also a place of business transaction and legal dispute settled by city officials.

Jesus unequivocally told Peter that the gates of hell should not prevail against the church. Listen to C. P. Wagner as he underscores this idea in his commentary on Matthew 16.

> *Jesus did not tell his disciples that their task was to build His Church without first warning them of the spiritual warfare it would entail. He said, "I will build My church, and the gates of Hades shall not prevail against it."* —Matthew 16:18
>
> *He didn't say that the gates of Hades wouldn't do whatever they could to hinder the growth of the Church; He just said they wouldn't prevail.*
> —Acts of the Holy Spirit by C. Peter Wagner

The gates of hell are hung on the entrance to the underworld. This Scripture gives obvious offensive encouragement. If we tenaciously pursue our enemy, we can prevail over his most vulnerable defense—the place of his illegal gate of entry and the place of our legal jurisdiction. Remember, we are to operate as "a church without walls," and the devil is hiding behind a facade that has been inadequately fortified. We can settle the dispute over spiritual authority by using the blood of Jesus to attack the gate of the enemy. The blood of Jesus provides the legal means to take back from the devil what we gave to him in the Garden of Eden, namely, control over the gate.

If we attack in the power of God's might, we will prevail. Some people may be afraid of a snake, but in reality a snake is more afraid of a human being. The same is true with mice. Upon confrontation, who do you think is more frightened, the mouse or the man? My wife would say the man, but the mouse is probably much more frightened. We are on the defensive because of fear.

The devil is really on the defensive, but through deception he tries to make us think we are. He is more afraid of us than we are of him. The devil is no match for us as believers if we activate what we have already been given. That's why he works overtime to convince us that we are inadequately equipped.

All Dressed Up and Nowhere To Go

Do you remember attending one of those Friday afternoon pep rallies in preparation for the high school homecoming football game ... the excitement and energy ... the band and the fired-up speeches? Remember the noise as the cheerleaders led shouts of victory?

More than an excuse to get out of class, these Friday afternoon pre-game frenzies had a purpose. They were supposed to provide inspiration and vision which could be translated from the pep rally to the playing field. Imagine if the team, with all equipment on, stayed in the pep rally or remained in the locker room because the coach kept drawing scenarios on the marking board. While preparation is imperative, games cannot be won with Xs and Os on the marking board. These may be safe and exciting aspects of preparation but, without an opponent to confront, there is no possibility of victory or defeat.

> Imagine if the team, with all equipment on, stayed in the pep rally or remained in the locker room.

How tragic when Christians are content to only "dress the part" and stay in the "pep rally" (sounds like a church service). Some soldiers wear spiritual armor but fail to use it. Wearing the military equipment of Ephesians 6 but not using it is the Christian version of "all dressed up but nowhere to go." There may be places to go but without prayer we suffer a detachment from God that results in unenergized soldiers with deactivated armor . . . armed but not dangerous.

The religious sect of the Pharisees in the New Testament exemplified this principle. They worked overtime at external appearance but

Jesus described them as dark, black sepulchers on the inside. Painted and pretty on the outside but dead on the inside, they were all dressed up and nowhere to go.

Paul instructs Timothy to warn against people who, in the last day, have a form—just an external appearance of godliness, but deny the power of God. The church cannot afford to be satisfied with a semblance or outward display of progress.

The correction to the Corinthians should suffice as an admonition concerning the proper balance between the inside and the outside (see 1 Corinthians 14). The church of Corinth had been marvelously equipped with the Holy Spirit, but they were not appropriately using their spiritual gifts.

Like electricity is a source of warmth and light to modern man, so were the spiritual gifts to the Corinthians. Like electricity, spiritual gifts if misused or not properly insulated can be powerfully destructive. The proper handling of spiritual gifts can be made possible through the insulation of wisdom and discretion. Spiritual gifts employed without proper administration can bring destruction.

> How tragic when Christians are content to only "dress the part" and stay in the "pep rally" (sounds like a church service).

Too often the gifts meant to enhance our private lives and our corporate meetings can be destructive because of misuse. Not only were believers not being edified but worse, unbelievers were leaving church services because of poor administration of these gifts. The gifts were not the problem. Poor administration of the gifts was the problem.

To exaggerate the inward work of the Spirit by an inappropriate external display does not edify the believer or the unbeliever. To think that we can scare people away from the cross by the misuse of spiritual gifts is quite sobering. Sometimes instead of killing the enemy, we kill the prisoners of war we were sent to rescue.

Wrong Equipment; Right Reason

When considering our spiritual struggle we must give serious consideration to the equipment and armor needed. The following possible problems, inherent to all Christians, should be addressed.

Number one: a soldier can have no armor (completely unarmed). Possible problem number two: a soldier can have correct armor and just not use it. Possible problem number three: can the soldier have the wrong armor altogether? This scenario is like David trying to use King Saul's armor.

The first perspective is ridiculous. No soldier would agree to go into battle without proper protection. The second possibility is a little more difficult. What must be done with a soldier who has the proper equipment but can't or won't use it? The third potential problem is the most difficult because some think they are receiving proper protection but, instead, have been covered with man's tradition. Tradition can be defined as something that once constituted proper application of truth. Our discussion here will be limited to the last two possibilities.

Is it possible to be armed with the wrong equipment yet be engaged in the right battle for the right reason? What a soldier wears into battle can determine the outcome. The uniform of a soldier must be appropriate for climate, terrain and culture and, for obvious reasons, weight, color, fabric, and fit must also be considered.

In this book we will study the protection provided by what we wear into battle. For the ancient military man, we called it armor; for the modern Christian soldier, we can call it the same.

The appropriate Christian outfit is essential. Often what we wear provides little protection and may not be suitable for battle. It might be heavy, cumbersome, outdated or entirely incorrect, given the current spiritual climate or culture. It is imperative for us not to mix new and old garments, for the new pieces applied to the old will make both ineffective (see Mark 2:21).

Is it not time to lay down some outdated armor picked up and put on along the way? King Hezekiah ordered the brazen serpent destroyed because its purpose of saving lives had been fulfilled nearly four centuries prior (see 2 Kings 18). He said it presented a "high place" and he called it "Nehushtan" (bronze thing). The children of Israel, because of a false sense of security and sentimental allegiance, failed to remove the symbol of the past—even though its effectiveness had long been removed.

We must not be satisfied with the counterfeit, thinking we have the real. Pride, tradition, self and many other accumulated, simulated pieces of armor need to be removed. Sometimes what we highly value and esteem, the King calls "just a brass thing." Don't go to battle with old, stale, worn-out faith. Spiritual "hand-me-downs" will not bring victory. Our Commander-in-Chief wants to custom fit us with new, appropriate apparel suitable for conflict, required for conquest.

Saul's Armor Doesn't Fit

There seems to be an ongoing conflict between what we are told to wear and what we feel adequate wearing. The suggested and recommended military attire may not fit you. As King Saul's armor-bearer, David was very familiar with the armor of the king, yet he had not proven it for himself.

He could not have confidence in Saul's armor to provide any personal protection or benefit. He had proven, however, a close relationship with Jehovah God built on praise and prayer. David's ammunition of worship and intercession could be used to defeat any spiritual enemy.

Although traditional battle armor may have been effective for Saul, the Scripture reports that David could not even walk in the borrowed armor, much less fight. Remember, David was called a man after God's own heart. He had a great plan for protection . . . a staff instead of a sword, and a sling in place of a spear. This afforded him great spiritual protection. This is amazing! When dealing with an enemy of this magnitude, you must know and trust spiritual techniques tested and proven effective . . . prayer and praise.

When considering the entire account of David's dealing with Goliath, from his initial contact to the final blow, he exhibits an important military approach—David stayed on the offensive! I believe this was the result of prayer, praise, and the anointing from Samuel, the prophet of the Lord, to be the next king of Israel (see 1 Samuel 16:13).

Regardless of the years that passed before David would actually occupy the throne as king, he operated under the influence of the anointing. The text states, "from that day forward David was anointed." Although the anointing will not always be obvious, it is always in operation. This should bring confidence and inspiration for us to stay on the offensive.

> David was called a man after God's own heart. He had a great plan for protection . . . a staff instead of a sword, and a sling in place of a spear.

The offensive posture of faith and confidence will also be misunderstood. David's brother Eliab accused him of being prideful and insolent of heart. Interestingly, within the text we find no indication of an offensive stance from Eliab, David's other brothers, or from their fellow soldiers. In fact, it is quite the opposite (see 1 Samuel 17:24).

Saul also misunderstood the victory of David, for the Scripture tells us that from this day forward Saul eyed David with suspicion (see 1 Samuel 18:9). Remember, the Spirit had already fallen on David "from that day forward." Thankfully, Samuel's anointing of David prepared him for Saul.

Notice a powerful principle found in 1 Samuel 17:51–53. Here we find a classic comparison between an offensive and defensive attitude. This profound principle illustrates the effectiveness of the anointing when moving from the defense to the offense.

> *Therefore David ran and stood over the Philistine, took his sword and drew it out of its sheathe and killed him . . . and when the Philistines saw that their champion was dead, they fled. Now the men of Israel and Judah arose and shouted and pursued the Philistines . . . Then the children of Israel returned from chasing the Philistines and they plundered their tents.*
> —1 Samuel 17:51–53

The entire text up to this point has illustrated the difference between the faith-filled actions of David and the fear-based inaction of his brothers. We have witnessed David's anointing inspiring him until he approached and attacked the enemy. His aggressive confidence, which resulted in victory, caused the entire enemy army to flee.

Conversely, we have watched a reluctant Israelite army on the defensive. Every day Goliath came out and shouted his challenge, but no one would answer the call. They were unable to respond to the antagonistic threats from Goliath because of lack of confidence and authority. However, notice the inspiring transition found in verse 52:

> *Now the men of Israel and Judah arose and shouted and pursued the Philistines.*

How could faith replace fear and action suddenly replace inaction? What was the inspiration behind this paradigm shift? What happened to turn David's men into an offensive threat?

Because of David's assertive attitude, godly reliance and inspired confidence, the armies of both Israel and Judah made the transition from a defensive posture—which had previously dominated every action—to an aggressive, offensive pursuit of the enemy.

The impact and influence of one anointed man or woman of God, energized by a cause, inspired by the Spirit, and activated through prayer and praise, cannot be overemphasized. Look what it did for

David, the army, and the general population. Everyone benefitted and received the reward of one offensive-minded military man.

Why Was David So Different?

The contrast between David and his brothers begs this question: What made David so different? David developed the reputation as a man of war much like his brothers, Eliab, Abinadab, and Shammah. However, the normal sibling similarities stopped there.

Nowhere do we find the brothers adding to their military prowess the art of praise and prayer like David did. Saul needed more than just military ability when looking for relief from emotional anguish and spiritual torment. The ability to play music skillfully was mentioned first as one of David's talents and I believe this set him apart from the other prospects! It gave him the ability to wage both physical and spiritual battles. Praise and prayer are major components that help accomplish victory on both levels.

In Psalm 149, David said high praises could be used to:

Execute vengeance on the nations, and punishments on the people; to bind their kings with chains and their nobles with fetters . . . to execute on them the written judgment.

We know that prayer and praise made David's heart alive. I believe this set him apart from every other warrior, especially his brothers. He warred with worship as well as the natural elements of warfare. While David's brothers were *armed but not dangerous*, David was armed with the name of Jehovah—and very dangerous!

God's government includes a department of defense and a department of offense. An offensive and defensive approach is imperative. We must do something. We can wear available armor, but to win, we must act. As Christian soldiers, it's time to activate the armor and become accomplished authorities in strategic maneuvers of spiritual warfare—both defensively and offensively. It is time for us to become "Armed and Dangerous!" It is time to pray!

— CHAPTER TWO —

PROTECTED BUT NOT PRODUCTIVE

ACTIVATING THE FIRST PIECE OF SPIRITUAL ARMOR THROUGH PRAYER

LOINS GIRD ABOUT WITH TRUTH

Stand therefore having girded your waist with truth. Pray always with all prayer.

—Ephesians 6:14, 18

The Scriptures declare a mandate for maturity and productivity. Abundant examples of growth, progress and maturity can be found in the general tone of the Bible and in the specific teachings of Jesus.

Phrases like "increase and abound in love," "let us go on to perfection," "that you may grow thereby," "being fruitful in every good work," "press for the mark of the prize," "grow up in Him," "that ye may be complete and entire, wanting nothing," "that you may be complete in every good work," "you shall be perfect," "you may abound to every work," "that you can increase more and more," and "that your faith grows exceedingly" are examples of the emphasis that the Bible places on progress. These and many other statements in Scripture strongly support the fact that we are required to be fruitful.

Even in the beginning, we find a charge given to Adam and Eve to excel and advance (see Genesis 1:8). God's blessing upon Adam and Eve was followed by a challenge to be physically productive and spiritually dominant. Let's take a closer look at the charge given to them!

1. Be fruitful (bear fruit)
2. Multiply (to increase)
3. Replenish (to fill, to be full)
4. Subdue (*kabash*—conquer)
5. Have dominion (tread down, crumble)

God gave the same blessing and charge to Noah when he and his family exited the ark (see Genesis 9:1, 7). God told them to be fruitful and to be abundant.

The covenant blessing that God gave to the children of Israel further emphasizes the importance of being fruitful and productive. Because of their obedience to the commandments, His promise of fruitfulness and productivity remained very effective. In Leviticus 26, we find the following list of covenant promises given to God's people (see Leviticus 26:4–11).

1. Rain in season
2. Land yields produce

3. Trees yield fruit
4. Harvest and sowing cycles back to back
5. Eat bread until full
6. Victory over enemies
7. Respected by God
8. Made to be fruitful
9. Made to multiply
10. Covenant confirmation

According to Leviticus 26, we will be naturally and spiritually fruitful if we stay in covenant with the Lord, and we will produce a harvest in the proper season if we continue doing well (see Galatians 6:9). Just review the list of promises in Leviticus and praise the Lord for His favor on your life.

Location, Location, Location

Early in the book of Psalms, we find the principle of fruitfulness addressed. In Psalm 1:3 we find blessing followed by a promise of fruitfulness, prosperity, and productivity.

And he shall be like a tree planted by the rivers of water, that brings forth his fruit in his season and his leaf shall not wither and whatsoever he doeth shall prosper.

The writer of Psalms reminds us of this principle: faithfulness will always result in fruitfulness. Fruit will result when we "grow beside the right river." One must be planted in the correct location. Let's look at the results of being planted beside the rivers of living water.

1. Fruit in season
2. Leaf will not wither
3. Prosperity in all activities

Jeremiah suggests the same idea of blessing and fruitful productivity because of the proper planting (see Jeremiah 17:7–8). Some people put roots down in depression, strife and fear. Others let roots grow deep into unforgiveness, tradition, preconception, prejudice, and stubbornness. God wants to properly plant us to promote deep-rootedness, but often our unwillingness to surrender to His planting and subsequent pruning results in a weak harvest.

Fruit Is Always in Season

In Mark 11:12–14, we find a forceful scriptural mandate to be productive. In these three verses, Jesus illustrates the gravity of bearing fruit regardless of the season. He cursed a fig tree and caused it to dry up from the root because it had the appearance of fruit, but no real fruit. It looked good from a distance. Too many believers impress others from afar but don't make an impact up close.

In this story, a close inspection would reveal no fruit. Figs, sometimes hidden under the leaves, were not to be found. The fruit of a tree indicates production and the seed in the fruit represents reproduction. To be productive, and to make reproduction possible, is of paramount importance, even though sometimes the spiritual season does not support being fruitful or productive.

> Too many believers impress others from afar but don't make an impact up close.

When Jesus inspects our life, He wants to find fruit even if it seems to be out of season in our spiritual life cycle. What will Jesus find when He lifts up the leaf of your life? The external representation of leaves without producing figs exemplifies being "armed but not dangerous." Jesus will not leave a misrepresentation unchecked. He desires us to be armed and dangerous, fruitful and productive.

Because failure to be productive brings swift and severe judgment, we must use every possible spiritual advantage to be fruitful. This can be accomplished through prayer. In this chapter we will discuss how prayer can result in reaping a harvest in every season.

Fruitfulness and Faithfulness

Sometimes we try to justify our lack of fruitfulness with a consoling comment along these lines, "Well, at least I'm faithful." Fruitfulness and faithfulness are not two distinct concepts but one spiritual principle, each being the direct result of the other. Each one should impact and influence the other.

A careful study of Matthew 25:14–30 reveals a profound connection between fruitfulness and faithfulness. From this familiar parable of talents we can better understand the interdependence of these two words. Some spiritual observations from these Scriptures where three servant men received specific instructions regarding the administration of the master's property must be made.

The entire story emphasizes the importance of production. Notice the meeting with the servants' master, who came to settle the accounts. The settling of the accounts was really an inspection of the administrative ability of each servant. We note from verse 15 that the distribution of talents was commensurate to the ability level of the servants.

Therefore, the lack of result from the one-talented man was merely an excuse and did not truly indicate a lack of ability. He simply did not use his "one-talent" ability. The real reason for burying the lord's money was fear. Fear clouded his perception of the master to the point he thought him hard and uncompromising.

I personally think the indignation of Jesus would have been less severe if the servant would have tried to invest it, but lost all of it. The words "wicked," "lazy" and "unprofitable" used to describe this man pale in comparison to the punishment rendered.

He was stripped of what he had been given and was cast into outer darkness where there was weeping and gnashing of teeth. This judgment seems so severe for receiving one talent and then returning it. His only infraction was not returning more than he received. Using this simple standard as the criteria, we should evaluate our own spiritual productivity.

The descriptive terms given the other two servants reveal the excitement of the lord of the vineyard. When he heard their business report of fruitfulness, he called them "good" and "faithful." These terms show quite a contrast to "wicked" and "slothful" (lazy). The fact that both of these "faithful" men doubled their gifts and consequently received identical rewards indicates the size of the initial gift did not matter. What truly mattered was proper use of what had been given. The risk was not in displeasing the master because of loss; the real risk was in not even trying to gain more.

Remember, because these servants were fruitful, Jesus called them faithful. In order to qualify as faithful they had to assume some risk in doubling their talents by trading. But listen to the reward of these fruitful and faithful men:

Well done thy good and faithful servant; you have been faithful over a few things I will make you a ruler over many things. Enter into the joy of your lord.

Risk brought the reward. In order to hear the Lord say, "Well done," we must do well. This certainly will involve risk and effort, but the reward will be worth it. The reward of rulership (or change of status) is for our time on this earth and in the kingdom to come. All of this brings expanded apostolic influence.

We are called faithful because we are fruitful. We are not called faithful because of drive, determination, tenure or our power to persevere. Our fruitfulness will qualify us as faithful servants worthy of a reward—if we steward wisely.

Much like a stockbroker who takes the oversight of someone else's money and invests it for a return, we should steward our abilities and finances not to have a loss or just break even but to produce a profit.

Someone has said that people can be placed into one of three categories:

Risk takers

Caretakers

Undertakers

People either advance by challenging the status quo (risk takers), maintain a respectable level of mediocrity (caretakers), or preside over the burial of a dream or goal (undertakers). Risk takers, the most exciting and appealing group, share some common characteristics, writes Lee Strobel in his book, *God's Outrageous Claims.*

They (risk takers) envision potential gains and rewards, they courageously seize opportunities, they exploit chances to grow and expand their horizons. Sure, they consider the potential losses, but they're more than willing to overlook the downside if the end result is worth it.

Because you never know what you can do until you have to do it, you should be grateful when you are stretched spiritually. Being stretched beyond your limits must happen if you want to live a life of faith and prosperity. A life of spiritual adventure awaits the Christian willing to risk his or her talents, gifts, and abilities in ministry efforts.

Remember, in the parable of the talents the servants were rewarded and called faithful because of the risk they exhibited. Risk takers are always rewarded with expanded influence, increased potential, and personal satisfaction.

If you are ready to assume some risk in an otherwise faithless prayer life, take heart from this passage, because growth, maturity, and spiritual productivity can be your reward.

In short, the one-talented man had a total misunderstanding of seed-time and harvest (see Matthew 25:24). When he quoted Jesus, he completely missed it. He needed a revelation that Jesus would not violate this law of the harvest. In the kingdom we must remember everything starts small and ends big. What starts as a seed grows into a harvest. Jesus will not violate His own law by reaping where He has not sown, and He will not gather where He has not scattered.

Mature and Multiply

The blessings of the Lord upon Adam and Eve, Noah, Abraham and others were directly tied to commandments. Most often in the Scriptures, blessings are contingent upon obedience to the commandments which are associated with that particular blessing.

In the case of Adam and Eve and Noah, God clearly said the reason for the blessing was so they could fulfill the commandment to multiply. Abraham was blessed to be a blessing (see Genesis 12:2). These blessings were not arbitrary blessings unattached to contingencies or unaffiliated with principles of personal responsibility. They came for the purpose of maturity and multiplication. Growth and reproduction are the natural results of the blessing of the Lord on our life and ministry.

When God called Israel, He did not intend them to be an elite people smug in their calling to be a nation of priests. He called them to assist in the work of reconciling all nations back into a loving relationship with God.

Although some may have thought God was showing favoritism, His intentions became more obvious when He called the tribe of Levi to become priests because Israel, as a nation, had forsaken its calling. It has always been the heart of God to bless the world through the nation of Israel. They were blessed to be a blessing.

The developmental stages of a human illustrate this concept of maturity and multiplication. The following stages of a natural life illustrate spiritual life:

(1) infancy   (2) childhood   (3) adolescence   (4) adulthood

Life begins with infancy. This developmental stage encompasses the first two years of a child's life. Because nourishment and protection come from others during infancy, the main objective during this stage is survival. In our spiritual life, the parallels are obvious yet worth mentioning. As new babies in Christ, we can do little for ourselves. We are at the mercy of more mature and seasoned saints. Even apostle Paul said the responsibility of the stronger is to bear the infirmities of the weaker (new Christians).

Our rate of spiritual survival exponentially increases when we are covered with the protection of prayer. Spiritual parents and pastors provide this kind of prayer. And remember, growth and development have just begun during this stage.

The childhood stage of life development follows infancy, and the focus of childhood is learning. This very exciting period of development enhances the inquisitiveness of a child as he/she moves into more independent learning and investigation. This phase spans the years from age three to five.

In the natural life development process, adolescence follows childhood. This stage can be divided into two general groups: ages six to eleven and ages twelve to nineteen. In adolescence, the focus is self. Youth in this stage are naturally preoccupied with physical appearance. Adolescence encompasses years of selfish struggle and is possibly the most protracted and difficult; however, it leads to the most exciting life development stage in which the focus moves from self-awareness and introspection to reproduction.

The next development stage is adulthood. The goal of this stage is to produce offspring. To produce means to give birth, to bring into existence. While the focus of the previous stages is protection provided by others, in the adult phase emphasis is on maturity, morality and on being personally productive. The life development process should always end in adulthood and reproduction.

In keeping with the biblical terminology, we must mature so we can multiply and replenish the earth. If our spiritual development does not result in the reproduction of spiritual children, we have not truly matured. True maturation must result in reproduction and praying in the Spirit with all prayer and supplication according to Ephesians 6:18. This helps make reproduction possible.

> More quickly and efficiently than any other exercise, prayer can move us from the preoccupation with being protected to a position of productivity and fruitfulness.

Pray For Reproduction, Not Just Protection

More quickly and efficiently than any other exercise, prayer can move us from the preoccupation with being protected to a position of productivity and fruitfulness. Remember, in order to ensure spiritual success we must become more offensive-minded. Because the church has settled into an unhealthy pattern of protection, often we have become so busy striving for survival that we miss many offensive opportunities for reproduction.

Just as in the natural life development cycle in which the emphasis of infancy is survival, sometimes spiritually we are stuck in a survival mode. Often, because of our lack of spiritual maturity, we accomplish little. We should not be satisfied with merely surviving, when the Bible declares our abilities sufficient to accomplish exploits for the kingdom of God. The incessant attacks from the enemy have reduced our definition of spiritual success from exploits to mere existence. The ultimate objective of every Christian should be to excel in spiritual adventure, not maintain mediocrity. We can advance into battle, not just complain about the attacks from the enemy. The survival mindset has robbed the church of the promise of procreation. We are not, with overwhelming results, making a difference to the kingdom of darkness. In the natural, the result of maturity is the physical ability to give birth, and the result of spiritual maturity should be the birth of spiritual babies being added to the kingdom of God.

PRAYER AND EVANGELISM

Somewhere along the path of progress, prayer and evangelism got separated. Jesus makes a compelling case for reconnecting the two.

> *Then He said to His disciples, "The harvest truly is plentiful, but the laborers are few. Therefore pray the Lord of the harvest to send out laborers into His harvest."* —Matthew 9:37–38

Prayer will yield a harvest of new births. Prayer was the prerequisite to Pentecost, and because of waiting in the Upper Room in unity and prayer, this regularly scheduled religious holiday became the launching pad for a tremendous evangelistic thrust that kicked the great commission into full gear.

Please notice this passage indicates no problem with the harvest, but it declares the harvest is plentiful. We have blamed our lack of a fruitful and productive harvest on a shortage of yield or difficulty of reaping. This is not valid. The problem lies with the labor force, and prayer can help rectify this. In this passage we find no shortage of fruit to harvest—just a shortage of prayer and compassion.

> The incessant attacks from the enemy have reduced our definition of spiritual success from exploits to existence.

This commentary on compassion sets up the story of the harvest. The reason for the shortage of spiritual babies is a shortage of laborers, and the reason for the shortage of laborers is a shortage of prayer; but the reason for the shortage of prayer is a shortage of compassion. Do we operate with a heart of compassion? Jesus had a heart for the harvest.

I wonder why this compelling compassion of Jesus doesn't move the heart of the church? When fueled (or inspired) by the compassion of the Lord, prayer can be used as a means of reproduction once we have developed a heart for the harvest. The Scripture assures us that when we travail in prayer, children will be born.

Few Christians realize prayer plays such an important part of the Great Commission. Luke's account suggests that the baptism of the Holy Spirit came because of prayer (see Luke 24:46–49).

This is no insignificant inference to prayer, but a powerful part of the Great Commission. Prayer is also mentioned here as a prelude to Pentecost, and in the book of Acts we see the obedience of the disciples displayed (see Acts 1:14).

Acts 2 vividly describes the birthday of the church. Intimacy inspired the birth, and prayer provided the power that produced the birth! These prerequisites for spiritual reproduction must also be evident in our lives. And the prayer process was vitally important in the discipleship of the new believer. According to Acts 2:42, after they received the Word and were baptized, they continued in prayer.

Protected But Not Productive

In Ephesians, we find a detailed description of a battle-ready soldier. He is fully armed with standard Roman military equipment. Ephesians 6:14 lists the first piece of armor.

"Gird your waist with truth."

Remember, this protective waist-wear covers the areas of the body that contain the power of procreation. The King James language uses a word critical to procreation: *loin*. In Ephesians, we have the picture of a soldier with the reproductive area protected.

We should rejoice in the sustaining power of God because He can keep us by preparing a table before us in the presence of our enemies—for this we celebrate. Even when under heavy attack, the power to procreate remains protected. However, if all reproductive capabilities are fully functioning, why so few children? Why so little fruit of the womb?

In one selfless prayer, Jesus moved His ministry into full maturity and exemplified moving from the adolescence stage—where the focus is self, to the mature stage of life development—where the emphasis is on reproduction. His prayer in the Garden of Gethsemane contains the key to spiritual reproduction. "Not my will, but thine be done," illustrating the style of sincere prayer that will move one from the adolescent stage of self into the mature stage of reproduction.

The single factor in our salvation is the cross, and Jesus' prayer precipitated the crucifixion. We can be born again because Jesus moved into full ministerial maturation by praying this prayer. He knew that unless a corn of wheat falls into the ground and dies, it would abide alone; but if it dies, in the soil of selflessness, it would bring forth much fruit (see John 12:23).

We were redeemed, bought back, and born again because of Calvary, so we could grow into adults capable of reproduction.

If, in adulthood, we stay on the spiritual defensive, we might be protected but will not be producing any spiritual children. Remember, the reason for the redemption afforded at Calvary was spiritual reproduction. Let's call it reproductive redemption—bought back to bring forth! The Garden prayer helped activate the girdle of truth until reproduction through Calvary resulted. In one triumphant prayer, the blood of Jesus dropped to the ground to irrigate the seed of God. Because of this, it brought forth much fruit!

> If the private prayer of Gethsemane made possible the public display at Golgotha, we should take heart in our private prayer struggles.

As with Jesus, prayer can activate your armor and move you from the defensive to the offensive. This may seem like an impossible proposition, but through prayer new territory can be taken and new battles won. If the private prayer of Gethsemane made possible the public display at Golgotha, we should take heart in our private prayer struggles. They will bring victory!

If the goal of adulthood is reproduction, we should ask ourselves with whom should we be intimate. Just as the natural result of a loving, intimate, mature relationship between a husband and a wife yields children, spiritual results should be no different. Remember, the armor around our waist, the girdle of truth, provides protection against the sterilizing power of error and allows spiritual reproduction through intimacy.

In order to activate the armor into a productive position, we must know the truth, and the truth will make us free. The meaning behind the word "know" is the key. The word *know* implies intimacy like Adam knew Eve, and children were born. In the original text, the Hebrew word *Yada* means "physical intimacy."

If we abide in a loving, intimate relationship with Jesus, who is Truth, we can and will be spiritually productive and fruitful. The armor, which protects us, must be the girdle of truth. With the proper relationship with truth, our armor can be activated until it is transformed into an offensive threat to the enemy.

If we would develop a love for the Lord until we move from *armed* (with the girdle of truth) *but not dangerous* to *armed and dangerous* because of our mature intimacy with Jesus, we could present the biggest threat ever to the devil. A productive harvest will be the result, and this happens because prayer becomes a priority. Our relationship with the Lord through prayer will result in reproduction.

Remember, we have been saved and are being sanctified. Sanctification has a duel application: set apart from sin and set apart to God. We are separated from the devil and his ways and we are separated to God to accomplish the intimacy needed for reproduction.

The heart of God remains: to protect for a reason... reproduction. He took His people out of Egypt (curse of slavery) so He could take them into Canaan. He blessed them so they could be a blessing. We must understand these stages of spiritual growth... cursed, blessed and becoming a blessing to others.

Prayers for Productivity Get Answered

Traveling as an evangelist presented my wife and me with many enjoyable and challenging times on the road. We learned the faith and tenacity needed to build a ministry and learned how to appreciate humble beginnings.

After years of diligent effort, we had established a comfortable ministry, preaching at mostly familiar places where there would be no "surprises." Our ministry had become protected by a predictable schedule, familiar places and comfortable pay. I also felt protected by the belt of truth securely in place around my personal study habits and preaching themes. I used truth for protection from theological or behavioral error, yet I longed for more productivity.

During a meeting in St. Louis, I felt such a stir in my spirit to increase spiritual productivity, I prayed an unusual prayer for an evangelist. As I put my scheduling calendar down on the communion table, knowing that my preaching was protected but not productive, I prayed:

"Lord, I'm tired of going where I want to go. I know where I can get treated right and paid well, but send me, Lord, where You want me to go! My schedule, this calendar, is Yours. Use me like never before to accomplish exploits for the kingdom of God."

I continued to pray for the will of God to be reestablished in my ministry, and what happened the next morning proves, without a doubt, that God answers selfless prayers for productivity. The phone calls started coming in; but instead of providing schedule additions with invitations from great churches, the next eight weeks of speaking engagements were erased from my calendar. Because of cancelled meetings, our budget was going to take a serious beating. These were meetings that had been scheduled for months.

I remember the sinking feeling as pastor after pastor, for legitimate reasons, asked to be excused from their commitment. This would have been more troublesome, had I not remembered the faith I felt the night before as I prayed the "not-my-will-but-Thine-be-done" prayer.

This example may pale in comparison to Jesus' "not-My-will-but-Thine-be-done" prayer in the Garden of Gethsemane. But I believe it illustrates how we need to surrender our human will to the divine purposes and become more mature and productive even in the little things. Our "Gethsemanes" may not be as dramatic as the one Jesus faced. Yet, we need them to complete the transformation to productive soldiers in God's army.

The productive outcome for Jesus, because He prayed in an attitude of surrender, is well documented—healing, salvation, victory and deliverance through the cross. The outcome of my "surrender prayer" in St. Louis was far less dramatic, yet for me it was productive.

We never missed one day of preaching or making our payments. The weeks filled in according to God's timetable and the results exceeded any of our previous meetings. I believe I walked in a greater anointing of the Holy Spirit and more personal confidence because of the surrender of my will.

When your will gives way to the will of God, more souls are saved, people healed, and spirits delivered than could ever be done from a safe, protected position of your own agenda. Pray the following prayer to become productive while protected.

Prayer Principle #1:

Prayer Principle of Maturity: Deals With Selfishness

The belt of truth is the protective prayer over the ability to spiritually reproduce. Pray this prayer in order to transition into a mature Christian—ready to surrender to God's plan of spiritual reproduction.

Our dear Heavenly Father, you have chosen it, and I will wear it. I put on the belt of truth. I pray a belt of truth around my waist. May I be protected from every enemy sent to destroy the powers of spiritual reproduction that I have been blessed with.

Your Word is truth and it protects me from error and false doctrine. Thank You, Jesus, for the protection made possible through truth.

Because the Bible instructs us to buy the truth and not to sell it, I pray this belt is so secure it will never fall off from neglect, be pulled off in battle, or be stolen while I'm resting.

By faith, I put on the belt of truth for protection from lies, deception, and even exaggerations. Not one false report or false accusation will penetrate the protection of truth.

Thank You for Your example. While in the Garden of Gethsemane You prayed a prayer of sacrifice that moved You into full maturity. Lord, make me mature. I pray my ministry would move into a deeper level of maturity through a similar prayer of sacrifice. Make me adult-like in my thoughts and actions as I continue to surrender to Your plans and purposes for my life.

I pray Your will would supersede my will. Dear Lord, help me to shift the focus from my selfish ambitions to a selfless desire to be faithful and fruitful. Thank You for the grace and power to transition into this profound place of surrender. May a real relationship of intimacy develop until responsible spiritual reproduction is the result. Lord, help me with protection and productivity. In Jesus' name. Amen.

Two point prayer plan:

1. Start praying now
2. Never stop praying

— CHAPTER THREE —

PROTECTED BUT NOT PASSIONATE

ACTIVATING THE SECOND PIECE OF SPIRITUAL ARMOR THROUGH PRAYER

THE BREASTPLATE OF RIGHTEOUSNESS

Having put on the breastplate of righteousness.
. . . praying always with all prayer.
—*Ephesians 6:14b, 18*

HEART PROTECTION

The second piece of the armor listed in Ephesians, chapter 6, is the breastplate of righteousness. Why did Paul say to put on the breastplate of righteousness? In Semitic cultures the heart (as well as other vital organs) represents the center of a man's being. Literally, a breastplate provides protection for both circulatory and respiratory systems of the human body. The obvious spiritual parallels are interesting and important.

While the word *righteousness* in this verse comes from a Greek word that includes integrity, virtue, generosity, piety, godliness or right living, the word *breastplate* comes from the Greek word *thorax*. In the study of human anatomy, the thorax represents the chest area from the neck to the abdomen. Like a soldier needs physical protection for heart and lungs, we need protection for our spiritual heart and lungs.

Jesus' blood flowing into our heart and His oxygen (breath) represent two functions vital to our spiritual survival. Please think it no insignificant coincidence that the New Testament refers to the Holy Spirit as our breath.

Righteousness can apply to our life at two levels: positionally and experientially. In one sense, according to the apostle Paul, we have been made the righteousness of God in Christ. This is positional. We are in right standing with God. On the other hand, we find Paul continually calling Christians to a higher, more holy and righteous life; this comes as the result of experience. We have positional righteousness by the grace of God but we must apply righteousness in order to live an overcoming, holy life.

We were made righteous by virtue of the fact that the penalty of sin has been paid, but presently we are being made righteousness as we experientially appropriate righteousness (right standing). Paul, when describing the soldier in Ephesians 6, indicates our responsibility to put on the breastplate of righteousness so as to experience victory.

How can we apply and activate this piece of armor? Maybe we should start by praying, according to the Lord's Prayer, for God to keep us from temptation and from evil.

Both the imputed righteousness of God and our application of His righteousness by living in right standing can provide protection for our heart. With a protected heart, we can serve God and live life with a sense of freedom, joy, purpose and passion.

Where has our passion and purpose gone? Perhaps God's righteousness and my right living, both of which are needed to protect my heart from being a wounded heart, have been missing. The breastplate of righteousness protects our personal purity and promotes passion and purpose.

Josh McDowell tells a story that illustrates how unrighteous living can damage your heart. After he finished teaching on sexual purity and abstinence, a pastor, who had brought his youth group to the meeting, came up to him and thanked him for the teaching. The youth pastor expressed how he knew it would help the kids, but then he gave this disconcerting report.

He said he and his wife, in three years of marriage, had never gone to bed alone; just the two of them. Josh said he was flabbergasted as he looked at a youth pastor who said he was taking his wife and multiple partners to bed.

The young man went on to explain. He said although he had repented and been forgiven for pre-marital sex with many partners, every time he and his wife went to bed he took the memory of those other women with them. He should have protected his heart from sexual involvement that allowed emotional and mental bondage. He should have used the breastplate of righteousness.

Protected From and Protected For

We should not only protect our heart from possible wounding but also protect it for the positive side . . . purpose and passion. A healthy spiritual heart is not so because of the absence of pain, but one that is empowered for the passionate and purposeful. We are not just trying to keep from falling; we are working to advance. We are not just trying to keep our hearts from being bruised by living in inactivity; we are working to live with passion and purpose.

The passion and purpose needed to conduct our secular and spiritual activities has been stolen. Too often our lives seem more habit than adventure and more boring than exciting. Passion springs from the heart, and the breastplate of righteousness protects the area of heart, lungs and other vital organs.

Yet, for many Christians, we are protected but not passionate or purposeful. For the sake of the Great Commission, the purpose must be an onward advance of the kingdom of God into the world of wickedness. The passion needed to accomplish this advance can come through prayer and praise.

David Did Not Fight with a Borrowed Breastplate

Please recall that our discussion is based on a soldier who had been issued a breastplate of righteousness to cover his thorax. In 1 Samuel 17, we are given two references to the protective covering for the thorax, with this interesting phrase used in verses 5 and 38: "coat of mail." The former reference is to the enemy Goliath and the latter to a shepherd boy named David.

Goliath's "coat of mail," as well as his bronze helmet, shin guards, and javelin, accompanied a fifteen-pound spear to make a complete suit of armor. However, in verse 38, the armor assigned to David, at the suggestion of Saul, was not suitable for a shepherd boy who had put his trust in Jehovah God. David soon realized this, as indicated when he said, " I have not tested these." He was saying that some men trust in horses, some men trust in chariots, but he would trust in the name of God (see Psalm 20:7).

David knew he would be no match for Goliath when wearing Saul's breastplate, so he traded in the breastplate borrowed from Saul and got supernatural protection. David pursued Goliath with a passion (heart) that was protected by something far better than Saul's coat of mail. I believe David had an invisible priestly outfit that came when Samuel anointed him to be king.

This kingly anointing inspired him to continue to praise and worship while fulfilling his responsibilities of shepherding the flocks for his father and while running from Saul. Apostle Paul, when describing David, quotes what God thinks of David: "I have found David the son of Jesse, a man after My own heart" (see Acts 13:22).

Even after the gross moral collapse of adultery and murder, David used repentance to renew his heart. His humility, along with praise and worship, must have helped David qualify as a man after God's heart in spite of human weakness. The sacred record reminds us: "Man looks on the outside, but God looks on the heart." God must have liked what He saw when He looked in David's heart.

I think David realized the premium God placed on the heart and he learned how to protect it through repentance, praise and worship. That helped prepare him to attack a giant like Goliath.

While engaging any enemy of Goliath-like proportions, like David we will be well equipped wearing our invisible priestly vesture of praise and prayer for protection. Remember, David wore his own breastplate, not Saul's.

Vance Havner writes that if the Israelites had waited until they could grow a giant as big as Goliath, they would still be pitched by the Valley of Elah. The answer was not in growing giants but in developing Davids who fight with a prevailing passion because of a covered heart. We are prone to overestimate our enemy and underestimate the protection of passionate prayer and praise.

> While engaging any enemy of Goliath-like proportions, like David we will be well equipped wearing our invisible priestly vesture of praise and prayer for protection.

When launching a bold offensive of prayer or praise, it is imperative not to be bound by what others suggest is appropriate for use or wear. David tells us that Saul's armor would be more appropriate for a defensive military posture. However, David was better prepared with the seemingly harmless, yet spiritually productive, technique of a shepherd's sling. Goliath had armor . . . but David was armed!

The supposed security and safety of someone else's armor will not conquer any significant enemies in our lives. It might provide some protection during a defensive stance, but it accomplishes nothing offensively. What appeared to be an irresponsible and reckless approach to the obstacle (Goliath) was truly a fresh, faith-filled advance toward victory for David. He wore an invisible protective breastplate prepared through prayer and praise.

Priestly Duties of Praise and Prayer

When Peter writes to the Jewish believer in his first letter, he reminds them that they were a royal priesthood called to offer up spiritual sacrifices (of praise) acceptable to God. As a prototype of a New Testament priest, David was not unfamiliar with the required priestly vestures, including a natural breastplate.

The Old Testament high priest wore a gem-covered linen breastplate ten inches wide by ten inches tall. These stones represented the twelve tribes of Israel. The breastplate was also designed to carry the mysterious Urim and Thummim, stones that served as a symbol of the high priest's authority and jurisdictional discretion while in the Holy of Holies.

Under the Mosaic economy, the priests were a special class appointed to minister unto God on behalf of the people; they enjoyed privileges not shared by others. They had a nearness to Jehovah peculiar to themselves. Vested with an authority, they were permitted to do that which was not given to those they represented.

David, a symbol of a different order of New Testament kings and priests, used that authority and discretion when he entered the battle with Goliath. The breastplate of righteousness mentioned in Ephesians is more closely represented by the breastplate that covered David's heart, thereby giving him figurative respiratory and circulatory protection. His heart (passion) was protected by prayer and praise (see Psalm 22:26).

You and I can use the same spiritual authority over our enemies when passionate prayer and praise becomes the linen breastplate used to protect our heart. This is possible because at the cross a radical change transpired when the old priestly order ended and a new one was inaugurated.

An appropriate passage to illustrate how David protected his heart through prayer and praise is found in 1 Chronicles 29:17–19. As the offering of materials and money was being collected from the people, David offered a prayer that emphasizes the heart.

David's breastplate of righteousness resembles the garment of praise given by Jesus during His earthly ministry. In Isaiah, we find a reference to the garment of praise (see Isaiah 61:3). This could be an inference to the new order of the high priest instructed to affect a change in the lives of the people. Observe the list of changes when Jesus shows up to establish a new priestly initiative.

1. Good tidings preached to the poor (Isaiah 52:7)
2. Healing for the brokenhearted (Luke 4:18)
3. Liberty to the captives (Luke 4:18)
4. Freedom to the incarcerated (Luke 4:18)
5. Comfort to those who mourn (Isaiah 61:3)
6. Beauty given for ashes (Isaiah 61:3)
7. Oil of joy given to mourners (Isaiah 61:3)
8. Exchange of the garment of praise for the spirit of heaviness (Isaiah 61:3)

Jesus began His ministry by going to the synagogue on the Sabbath and quoting from Isaiah 61. Hinting at a radical departure of the old order of priestly protocol, Jesus disclosed His intentions to launch a new and different order of priests. David typified the new order of priests who would offer up praises unto God as a part of their priestly duties.

Under the new covenant, the sacrifice would be a living sacrifice of priestly praise and prayer instead of the bloody, lifeless body of a goat or sheep. You and I are New Testament kings and priests with the ministry of worship enabling us to offer a sacrifice of praise.

Priestly Protection While Attacking

Upon close observation of the priest's breastplate in the Old Testament, we find these words written, "upon his heart" (see Exodus 28:28–30). This was a linen breastplate suspended from the shoulders by golden chains and fastened to the girdle by blue lace. This covering for the heart may not have been necessary for battle with the enemy, but for proper placement of the names of the people to be represented in the presence of God it was vital.

Just as David's protection was more closely related to the breastplate the high priest wore, the protection over our spiritual circulatory and respiratory systems is prayer and praise. Prayer and praise protect us defensively, while simultaneously promoting a confidence to move to the offensive. Just like David, it is time for us to attack with confidence. I love the attack attitude of David found in the Psalms (see Psalm 149:6–9).

Here David displayed how passionately we can conquer and control the enemy who formerly manipulated us. We need to use this inspiring example to move into our New Testament ministry as priest. With the proper balance between guarding and gaining, between battling and building, between the offensive and the defensive, we will prevail. Our hearts can be protected yet passionate for the work of God. It is beautiful to note in the Song of Solomon what the Bride says to her beloved regarding a passionate heart that is sealed or protected (see Song of Solomon 8:6).

Intercession and Righteousness

In a reassuring passage, Pastor James, with no subtle inference, connects prayer and righteousness (see James 5:16). The line of logic in this verse bears investigation. Because a man is outfitted in the protective covering of (breastplate) righteousness, and then with passion and fervency prays, the prayer has much power. The man doesn't prevail as much as the prayer of the man prevails. The descriptive qualifier for the man in this verse is " righteous."

Prayer from one whose heart is protected by the breastplate of righteousness occupies no common place of power . . . it has much power. I believe the breastplate of righteousness is also what allowed, moreover inspired, the effectiveness of this prayer.

The righteousness of God in us cannot be accomplished in our own noble efforts of self-righteousness. The energy of the flesh does not cover our heart with the pristine linen breastplate of His royal righteousness, but enshrouds us with tattered, torn, filthy rags of human accomplishment and carnal wisdom (see Isaiah 64:6).

Prayer, Self-Righteousness and Religion

Jesus took on the unpopular topic of self-righteousness. Using a parable about a Pharisee and a tax collector, He spoke of "some who trusted in themselves that they were righteous" (see Luke 18). The context quickly reveals that the religious leader, the Pharisee, was smug and cocky regarding his prayer life.

> The energy of the flesh does not cover our heart with the pristine linen breastplate of His royal righteousness, but enshrouds us with tattered, torn, filthy rags of human accomplishment and carnal wisdom.

His "prayer" was really a resume of self-righteousness. In it, he recounts his distinguishable virtues, reminds God of how good and generous he is, and also lists all the low-life people that can't be compared to him. Wow! This guy was really religious; it came through loud and clear during his prayer time.

The tax collector, on the other hand, was humble and actually prayed to God for mercy as a sinner rather than bragging about being a saint. The righteousness of God (remember he went away justified) was the result of his prayer. The tax collector prayed with selfless humility and gained righteousness, while the religious man prayed with self-righteousness and got humbled.

The Pharisee found false protection from his "breastplate of self-righteousness" but the sinner who admitted being unprotected and vulnerable found true protection in the "breastplate of righteousness" given to him by God.

SELF-RIGHTEOUSNESS OR GOD'S GARMENT

The difference between man's righteousness and God's righteousness is the difference between a pauper dressed in filthy rags and a princess dressed in royal attire. We find this interesting simile used by Isaiah when he contrasts man's righteousness and God's righteousness (see Isaiah 64:3). He said the self-righteousness of man looks like filthy rags when contrasted to the royal righteousness of our great God.

> The difference between man's righteousness and God's righteousness is the difference between a pauper dressed in filthy rags and a princess dressed in royal attire.

We know God's righteousness comes to us, not because of what we wear or what we do, but is internally imputed to us and therefore cannot be self-righteousness. Man cannot be made righteous by his own actions, but through faith in the action of Jesus on the cross.

Righteousness, as a work of God's grace, must be accomplished on the inside of man. Consequently, in this verse we find a reference to the inadequacy of outside covering. Even when we try to tailor-make a good-looking garment of self-righteousness, it turns out like a rag. Only in a heavenly setting do we find righteousness externally obvious.

The apostle Paul, in his valedictory address, tells of a crown of righteousness waiting on him in heaven. Just think, God has given us a garment for the marriage supper in heaven and our earthly application of His righteousness makes possible this reward in heaven.

If righteousness should not be externally flaunted, why is the breastplate of righteousness in Ephesians 6:14 an external protection worn by warriors? If righteousness starts on the inside, how can the inside protect the outside?

True internal righteousness should form an impenetrable external covering. In keeping with our soldier, who wore a breastplate (outside) of righteousness (inside), this work of the Spirit can form a breastplate (protection) on the outside. If there has been no work of the Spirit on the inside of our hearts, there will be no real protective breastplate possible on the outside. The outside protection comes as a result of peace and purity on the inside.

People who have erected walls of defense around their heart for protection are reminiscent of King Saul's suggestion that David wear his (Saul's) breastplate. You can try to cover your heart with human effort or natural armor but true protection comes through the glorious covering of God's righteous breastplate.

I define self-righteousness as closed-heartedness. A self-righteous person is so smug they reject any outside idea or opinion and stay "closed" to any different thoughts or perspectives. Religious people, more than most, must guard against the false sense of security and protection that comes from a breastplate of self-righteousness. The devil delights in this deception. When we feel or look protected by our own righteousness, we actually close our heart to the very thing the Lord wants to put into us to protect us. This is classic self-righteousness.

As a result of this closed-heartedness, judgmental tendencies take over and detailed score keeping and list monitoring result. However, when we replace the "breastplate of self-righteousness" with the real "breastplate of righteousness," a freedom from the human tendency to keep records of injustices will result. Without a list of wrongs that need to be "righted," you are free to live within the protection of God's breastplate. Then, because of a healthy heart, one is free to push past just being protected into passionate progress.

This inside job of righteousness results in internal integrity. Integrity comes from the mathematical term *integer*. An integer is a number which cannot be divided and therefore maintains equity and wholeness. Our own righteousness must fade and be replaced by sound, indivisible righteous character, which only comes from the Lord. Then we can have internal integrity.

When His righteousness covers us, we become not only protected, but also passionate and purposeful. Remember, the protection of a breastplate affords little offensive capabilities until the soldier becomes passionate regarding the purpose of destroying the devil.

Robes to Rags

When I felt the Spirit tell me to interrupt the Sunday morning worship service and make an appeal for salvation, it scared me. Before I could employ human reasoning or judgment, I boldly declared, "If anyone will come right now to this altar, God will save, deliver, and fill you with the Holy Spirit." Only seconds had passed when a first-time guest hit the aisle and came forward. It was a glorious, genuine, powerful conversion and deliverance. The gentleman was completely set free from years of drug addiction, instantly delivered from withdrawals, and physically healed. Years of drug use had destroyed his olfactory senses, but they were miraculously healed that morning. It was a special Sunday morning service.

The miracles that followed were almost as dramatic. The favor of God, as well as favor from men, seemed to flow uninterrupted to this new believer. For example, a drastic decision, unprecedented in the courts, reduced a prison sentence from 75 years to 2 years.

This man truly represented the healing, deliverance and overcoming power of God. He seemed to grasp and quickly apply spiritual principles. His evangelistic efforts yielded many new converts and sparked church growth. He and his wife became a respected and productive part of our local church family and remained so for a number of years.

The behavior that followed seemed so far from the man True Life Church had grown to love that, for an inordinate length of time, it was overlooked and ignored. He went from suggesting that the pastor was fighting temptation with men, women, and money to telling paid staff, and many others, that church attendance and tithing were under the law and totally unnecessary.

He went from conducting home meetings designed to undermine pastoral authority, to defending people of questionable moral character who the elders were disciplining. These examples represent many things so unexpected from one of our favorite sons.

Unfortunately, the harm and spiritual setback from this one situation caused more pain and heartache than anything I have had to deal with in 26 years of ministry. How could this be? Where did things go wrong? How could this man become so unteachable while pretending to be teachable? How could he be privately closed-hearted while appearing publicly to be so open? Was self-righteousness now replacing God's righteousness? The predictable outcome of closed or wounded-heartedness follows a pattern witnessed by countless spiritual leaders.

Breastplate of Self-Righteousness

The presumed protection that comes from closed-heartedness (self-righteousness) is so deceiving. When one thinks he/she is vindicated and justified, and sets their heart toward that predisposed opinion, there comes a hard, impenetrable covering that feels like a breastplate of righteousness, when in actuality it is a breastplate of self-righteousness.

The false security that comes from a heart that is wounded or wicked thus hardened toward correction or change makes a person feel safe and protected. At this point they become most vulnerable, not protected.

The heart of David (remember he was called "a man after God's own heart") was antithetical of the man from our church. David, even when he had legitimate reasons to turn on Saul, respected the position and authority of Saul. David had every human reason to become closed-hearted and self-righteous because of how Saul had treated him. When he could have responded out of a wounded heart, he stayed protected by prayer and praise and acted admirably toward Saul. David truly found the breastplate of righteousness to be a deep work inside his heart, as exemplified by his external display of prayer and praise.

Like any minister who has invested twenty-six years in full-time ministry (twenty of which I have been pastoring the same church), I have seen too many believers start out open-hearted and teachable, only to become bitter, closed-hearted, and unteachable.

I can report from experience that the depth of devilish deception can find free and easy access through the supposed security of self-righteousness! Regrettably, in some instances, the progression for some who start out sincere follows this three-part pattern.

As new believers, people have a teachable, open and hungry heart. They want to learn and, because they are babies, they are somewhat dependant on others to teach them. Also, the breastplate of righteousness will protect them. Because these folks generally are unlearned in religious protocol and tradition, I call this stage the "Unreligious Spiritual." These people are more spiritually hungry than they are religiously satisfied. At this stage they are protected but not productive. In the New Testament, Paul refers to this group as babies.

As these babies become more mature, they grow into the best and most productive stage. Paul refers to people in this category as "spiritual." I call them "Spiritual Religious." The people in this group have a healthy balance between religious structure and spiritual freedom. This phase is the very best position for protection and productivity. These established, educated, seasoned saints are not dependant like the new believer in Phase One, but interdependent. They are mature and capable of mentoring and discipling new believers. They want to be taught so they can teach.

The third, and most unfortunate stage, Paul called carnal Christians in 1 Corinthians 2. I refer to them as "Religious Unspiritual." These are smug, closed-hearted, unteachable people. They become so religiously closed-minded, they think there is nothing more for them to learn. They allow the breastplate of righteousness, meant to protect their heart, to become a false protection of self-righteousness. The sad result is always the same; they become unprotected and unproductive.

I have witnessed, too often, sincere saints becoming closed-hearted when hit by the unsuspected enemy ammunition of self-righteousness. Self-righteousness is subtle because it begins in sincerity and it often goes undetected for a long time. It initially dresses in a legitimate outfit of God's righteousness before becoming contaminated by pride and an unteachable spirit. At this point, the robes of God's righteousness become the tattered, dirty rags of self-righteousness. Refer to the chart at the end of this chapter to further educate yourself with this pattern.

Prayer Principle #2:

Prayer Principle of Passion: Deals with Self-Righteousness

The breastplate of righteousness is the covering for the vital organs, particularly the heart. The heart speaks of passion. This prayer will help you discern the kairos timing of God's set season and revitalize your zeal for the kingdom.

Our dear heavenly Father,

Today, like every day, I get dressed for battle. Through prayer, I cover my heart with Your protective power. Like a breastplate protects the respiratory and circulatory systems of the human body, protect the spiritual systems inside of me. By faith, these systems are guarded and are safe.

Protect me from hard-heartedness, from becoming cold or indifferent, and from becoming calloused. I pray in Jesus' name that my heart is pure and undefiled, pliable and flexible. I apply the breastplate of Your righteousness. Take from me any self-righteousness and cover me until I can become Your righteousness.

I thank You for the power of prayer that helps me activate the breastplate. I have put on the protective covering of the breastplate of righteousness. Now turn it on through this prayer. Turn it on so I am not only protected but also passionate. With this activation, I advance into the things I have been called to do with confidence.

I pray to enter into a passionate heart of repentance. I repent of pride that would restrict recovery from sin. Activate the breastplate through Your righteousness. With a pure heart because of Your righteousness, I passionately advance into an offensive initiative that will destroy the enemy.

Through sincere prayer, priestly praise, and right living, activate my righteous protective covering. My heart will not go unprotected because of my self-righteousness. I know there is no battle protection with rags of self righteousness, but with the Breastplate of Righteousness protection starts on the inside and works out. Cover me now, I pray. Thank You, in Jesus' name. Amen.

TWO POINT PRAYER PLAN:
1. START PRAYING NOW
2. NEVER STOP PRAYING

Three Phases of the Breastplate

	1st Phase	2nd Phase	3rd Phase
Name	Unreligious Spiritual	Spiritual Religious	Religious Unspiritual
Survival	DEPENDENT Can't survive without help	INTERDEPENDENT Can't survive without each other	INDEPENDENT Won't survive
Knowledge Level	Teachable student	Teachable teacher	Unteachable teacher
Desire/ Motive	Want to learn	Want to learn so they can teach	Not learning yet teaching
Breastplate	Breastplate of righteousness (Faith)	Breastplate of righteousness (Proper balance of faith and works)	Breastplate of self-righteousness (Works)
Heart Protection	Protected but not yet productive	Protected and productive	Unprotected and unproductive
Heart Position	Openhearted	Openhearted and appropriately guarded	Closed hearted

— CHAPTER FOUR —

Prepared But Not Progressing

Activating the Third Piece of Spiritual Armor Through Prayer

Feet Shod with the Preparation of the Gospel of Peace

and having shod your feet with

the preparation of the gospel of peace.

Pray always with all prayer and supplication.

—Ephesians 6:15, 18

As Christian soldiers, our feet have been prepared with the gospel. This armor protects us during conflict and enhances our offensive advance. Because we are protected from the devil, we need not retreat but should go with confidence into spiritual conflict. Through the good news of the gospel we can move to an offensive position until our protected heel steps on the vulnerable head of the enemy.

Oh, the peril of not progressing. Every one of us should spend considerable time and effort evaluating our spiritual progress. If this journey is anything at all, it should be a pathway of progress. Advancement, movement, maturity, and adventure should describe our spiritual journey. How do you fare when measuring yourself against these milestones? But, as you are aware, our progress can be stalled when problems and pressure shake our spiritual footing.

The writer of Hebrews strongly stresses progress by abandoning the elementary principles and advancing to completion and maturity (see Hebrews 6:1). We must not simply go on to other things, but go on to higher things. As the text from Ephesians reminds us, life is not just a playground, but also a battleground. In order to be prepared to progress in spiritual warfare, we must forsake the security of the familiar and launch out in pursuit of new territory.

> If this journey is anything at all, it should be a pathway of progress. We must not simply go on to other things, but go on to higher things.

James Irwin, the first man in space, said, "You might think going to the moon was the most scientific project ever, but they literally threw us in the direction of the moon and we had to adjust our course every ten minutes, yet we landed just fifty feet inside a 500-mile radius of our target." To be worthy warriors in this spiritual war, we must launch out. We cannot become who we need to be by remaining where we are.

As Christians, we are on a flight of faith, going in the general direction of a heavenly reward. But, in order to stay on course and land within the target, in-flight adjustments and mid-course changes may be necessary. A Christian person or organization should not float aimlessly through space to some accidental landing. Every believer should most closely resemble a spaceship on a mission with a targeted destination.

What changes do we need to make to ensure spiritual progress and targeted landing? All of us resist change, yet the process of maturation demands adjustments and change. If we want to grow, we must change. We must become what the Creator intended us to be, and in order to accomplish this, we must always begin with the foundation.

Focus On the Foundation

The foot represents foundational truth, direction, and firm footing. In ancient warfare, the Roman soldier wore sandals with cleats to ensure firm footing. He realized that military victory required proper footwear designed not to slip. The foot also speaks of direction and mobility and, in the Scriptures, it always symbolizes conquest and victory. However, the most obvious symbolism is that of a foundation, the basis from which to build.

The description of the soldier in Ephesians 6 gives us an idea of the importance of the foundation when using the phrase *feet shod with the preparation of the gospel*. By understanding the meaning behind the word *preparation*, we see why the emphasis is placed on this part of the military attire. Remember, the foot suggests the foundation or basis.

When constructing a building, the first order of business is always the footing and the foundation because its strength determines the rest of the structure. Likewise, in our Christian fight we should have the proper basis. If the foot represents the foundation, there can be no standing without it. Furthermore, with the proper preparation and firm footing, we should be immovable in the time of battle.

To the Corinthians Paul said, *"no other foundation can anyone lay than that which is laid, which is Jesus Christ"* (see 1 Corinthians 3:11). The foundation is gospel salvation and the Word of God. But we must be careful how we build on this foundation. We have been given the gospel of peace for our spiritual footwear but we must learn how to use it. The distribution of military attire is the responsibility of the authorities, but the soldier must learn how to properly use the equipment. The Lord has given us the gospel of peace, but we need to use it correctly.

The foundation has been laid, not by us, but for us; yet we must advance the good news by using our legs and feet to walk out the gospel of peace.

Preparation of the Gospel of Peace

In order to stand firm, we must take time to prepare. The word *preparation* accurately translated from the original language means "readiness," and proper footwear makes the soldier ready for combat. Preparation is essential to any military campaign or spiritual adventure. That is why the apostle Paul underscored it in his letter to the church at Corinth (see 1 Corinthians 14:8).

Paul understood the power of preparation when he addressed the church at Corinth. However, the interesting idea about the military readiness of the soldier in Ephesians 6 is the combination of two contrasting concepts. On one hand, we see a soldier dressed in full armor ready for any enemy; on the other hand, we find he has been prepared for battle by equipping his feet with the gospel of peace. How can peace be a part of being prepared for battle? Let's look to Jesus.

When the prophet Isaiah tells of the coming Messiah, he describes Him by His name. His name shall be called *The Prince of Peace*—a name for Jesus only found in this passage. Isaiah clearly declared a time to prepare—to get ready—for there will be One born who will inspire a heavenly choir of angels to sing, *"Peace on earth and good will toward men."* Further, the idea of preparing for the coming of Jesus was the ministry theme for John the Baptist (see Matthew 3:3).

The process of preparation must include peace as a part of the armor. There was always a day of preparation for the Sabbath; remember, the Sabbath was a day of rest and peace. We must prepare for conflict with the gospel of peace. That seems like a contradiction but it is necessary for spiritual success. Take time today to shod your feet with the gospel of peace before the heat of the battle burns.

Isaiah brings clarity when he records these words:

How beautiful upon the mountains are the feet of him that preaches the gospel of peace. —Isaiah 52:7

PREPARED BUT NOT PRETTY

What does it mean to be beautiful or pretty? Often we equate beauty, in the most obvious application, as external appearance. Another familiar application of the word refers to the beauty of the inner man or beauty of the heart. My favorite application of this principle comes out of Psalm 48:2, where we find the words describing our great Lord as being *"beautiful for situation."*

Beautiful for situation, the joy of the whole earth, is Mount Zion on the sides of the north, the city of the great king.

In this verse, *beautiful* is not defined as pretty, but as timely or correct. It has the understanding of belonging to the right hour: *beautiful for situation.* When referring to His sense of timing and intervention, the Lord has no equal, and for this He should be praised greatly.

In keeping with the Ephesians 6 soldier, where we find the armor on but not activated, we sometimes are prepared or fitted with the correct equipment but we are not beautiful. Remember, *beautiful* means the precise point in time where a divine intervention transpires. Because we have not activated our spiritual armor by prayer, we are not operating our lives with any real sense of God's timing. We therefore do not belong to the right hour.

If, on our spiritual journey, we do not appropriate God's correct time, we may be prepared *(beautiful for situation)* but not pretty. We must know and trust the Lord implicitly, thereby waiting for His will and operating within the framework of His set season for us. How can you be assured of these things? Pray!

In a vivid description of Jesus, the prophet Isaiah foretells of a day when the messianic ministry of Jesus will be on the earth. In so doing, he chooses some interesting language. Paul quotes the same passage when addressing the church at Rome.

> *And how shall they preach unless they are sent? As it is written: How beautiful are the feet of those who preach the gospel of peace, who bring glad tidings of good things.* —Romans 10:15

Action associated with feet makes them beautiful. In this verse, they look beautiful because of the action of preaching. They are activated. As we have learned in the example of the Ephesians 6 soldier, prepared feet should be equated with the foundational aspect of the armor. The foundation is made beautiful or pretty (useful) when it is used to build upon. Paul stresses the importance of how to build when he admonishes the church not to build with wood, hay or stubble upon the glorious foundation of Jesus Christ (see 1 Corinthians 3).

Keep in mind, our goal is to activate the armor by prayer. When the foundation serves its purpose as a basis for a building, it becomes a part of that building. Prayer should be a part of our spiritual armor and a part of our spiritual building. It may not be the most obvious part, but it is the most important. The foundation is not the most glamorous or flashy part of a building, but there would be no building without it. Remember, the subject matter of Paul's sermon to the Romans was *"the gospel of peace"* (see Romans 10:15). That's why our feet should be shod with *the gospel of peace*.

Another great example of belonging to the correct hour through prayer is found in Acts 3:1–2. Here we find Paul and John prepared and also pretty, or beautiful, for the situation.

The name of the gate mentioned in this passage, *Beautiful,* is interesting because it has the same original language root as the word *hour* found in the same verse. Both words mean, "belonging to the right hour or season." For this lame man, the name of the gate is significant because his hour for a miracle had arrived. Paul and John told him they did not have any money to give him, but they did know One beautiful for every situation.

"In the name of Jesus Christ of Nazareth rise up and walk," were the words by which the lame man's foundation or basis was restored. Prayer and faith activated this man until now he had new spiritual footwear. Remember they had waited in the upper room in one accord in prayer until Pentecost. His feet were shod with the preparation (foundation) of the gospel of peace. Feet once immobile received healing through the timely ministry of Peter and John. That really is beautiful!

Beautiful and timely obedience to the Great Commission brings healing to our feet and anklebones so we can go and help others accomplish the same. The Lord wants to heal His body, the church, and He wants to restore strength to the area that supports the body.

Remember, the foot is the part of the body which determines direction, stability, basis and foundation. It also represents conquest and victory. We can subdue and trample every spiritual enemy, but we must first be healed. Little wonder Paul said to pray always, at every stage of spiritual armor application.

A seven-day prayer meeting in Acts 2 precipitated the Pentecostal outpouring where Peter and John, and 118 others, received power that prepared them for the ministry demands when dealing with a crippled man. Likewise, prayer and Pentecostal power should empower us to help deliver people, churches and ministries from paralysis. They prayed to go and then ministered to a lame man while going to pray.

> The foot is the part of the body which determines direction, stability, basis and foundation. It also represents conquest and victory.

They were shod with the gospel of peace by waiting ten days and because of the infilling of the Spirit. The coming of the Holy Spirit listed in Acts 2 kicked the great commission into *beautiful* (timely, right hour) readiness as shown in Acts 3. When is the right time for a man to walk? In this story, beauty and timing were not in the man's need. He had been in need since his birth; beauty and timing were in the preparedness of the disciples.

Through prayer we can defeat crippling problems in the church because we see our problems in new faith-filled light. How many times had Peter and John walked by the lame man, but after being prepared with the gospel on their feet, they walked in God's perfect timing and looked at a lame man through the eyes of the Healer. They were shod . . . they were ready. Their feet were strong, and now the crippled man's feet were also made strong.

Confusion Means Instability

When the disciples were not prepared, it resulted in confusion. The gospel according to Mark renders an account of a man who came to the disciples for the deliverance of his son, but they failed at the man's request. Jesus challenged their unbelief and reminded them: *"this kind can come out by nothing but prayer and fasting."*

Jesus declared a powerful principle: the problem was not with the man or his son. The unpreparedness was not in the man, for he said, *"I believe, just help my unbelief."* Jesus shows us that honest faith can be used for miracles even if it is not perfect. The disciples were simply not ready. They were not right or timely. Confusion came as a result—confusion regarding the blame for this ill-fated attempt at deliverance—confusion and debate surrounding the overselling but under-delivering of the disciples.

The disease of confusion must be dealt with, for it has left us lame and mute long enough. The apostle tells the believers at Rome that God is not the author of confusion but of peace. *Confusion* comes from a Greek word meaning "instability or disorder." God did not originate instability or disorder; however, He did institute peace.

Pay special attention to the word *instability*. To overstate the obvious: *Instability,* the inability to stand on your feet, makes you unsure and susceptible. Through prayer, the Lord can heal the instability caused by confusion and in its place bring peace. The church can stand strong because of the prayer that prepares us, thereby promoting progress!

Increasing or Not Decreasing

The difference between playing to win as opposed to playing not to lose illustrates the contrast between playing offensively and defensively. The preparation may have been adequate, maybe even superior, but that does not ensure victory. We all can list people who seemingly are prepared but not progressing. The key to advancement and success in any endeavor is the proper application of preparation. Someone has edited an old saying to say, "Practice doesn't make perfect. Perfect practice makes perfect!" How we prepare and then how we apply what we have learned in that preparation is vital.

One must constantly resist the tendency to merely maintain or survive. It is not the will of the Lord for any person, ministry or church to just "not decrease." There must be increase. Some people have the idea that living for God is "not sinning." That's not living. It may be existing but not living. In the economy of God, I don't think we can consider "not failing" a success. The following comments are typical of the "at least we're not decreasing" mindset:

> In the economy of God, I don't think we can consider "not failing" a success.

Regarding marriage: "Well, at least we're not divorced."

Regarding work: "At least I haven't been fired."

Regarding finances: "I'm not bankrupt yet."

Regarding church: "At least I go to church."

Our walk with the Lord should be one of abundant living. That's why He came (see John 10:10).

To live life to the fullest, we must progress through the following four levels of living.

Existing: barely alive.

Experiences: past successes and failures.

Exploration: new possibilities.

Exploits: God's plan for our lives, present and future.

God's plan for His children includes increase and abundance regardless of past experiences or current environment. Paul adds these encouraging words: *"In all these things (trials and tribulations) we are more than conquerors through him who loved us."* Notice the location of the victorious conqueror—in the middle of troubling situations, not outside of them. The word *conqueror* defines somebody who came through a fight or struggle having prevailed against the opponent. A *more than conqueror*, however, reflects a person prevailing because of the preparation of the gospel of peace, even in the midst of difficulty.

> The key of increasing while decreasing may seem like an elusive oxymoron, but it transpires automatically when I do my part—decrease.

My increase and abundant living is directly linked to Jesus increasing in my life. John understood this concept. He said, *I must decrease and Jesus must increase* (see John 3:30).

The key of increasing while decreasing may seem like an elusive oxymoron, but it transpires automatically when I do my part —decrease. I can't bring the increase of God's love or grace. That is beyond the sphere of my spiritual privilege or responsibility. However I can be responsible for what I must do, namely the diminishing of selfish ambition.

"Increasing while decreasing" best describes God's will for every spiritual soldier. The comprehensive objective of the entire army must increase while the selfish ambition of the individual soldier must decrease. Likewise, *increase* is a team sport, even in our churches. The superstar status of one or two must decrease so the entire church can increase. If God's army increases over man's desire, the kingdom and the government of God will be established.

God's one-two punch of government and peace will bring the increase and will result in absolute abundant living.

The Increase of Peace

In Isaiah 9:7, we find a promise of the ever-increasing peace of God. When we read these verses of the increase of the government and the peace of God, we ask, "How can this happen?" The word *increase* gives us the answer. The Hebrew word for increase is *marbiyth* meaning "multitude or offspring." Because government and peace are two components of one promise, they are to be considered complementary and consistent, one with the other.

You cannot have the peace of God without the government of God, and the government of God brings peace. Thank God, the children of Israel didn't stop having children. By virtue of birth (offspring), not by election or having been overthrown, both the government of God and peace of God increased. This is precisely how God's government and His kingdom will increase today. Through the fulfillment of the Great Commission and birth of spiritual babies. Israel's government from the lineage of David also flowed forward until Jesus was born through the royal bloodline. This concept is heralded from heaven by an angel at the birth of Jesus (see Luke 2:14).

The Old Testament prophecy of the increase of peace found in Isaiah 6 is fulfilled in Luke 2, when God came in human form and lived on this earth. He was born a King with the express purpose of establishing His kingdom and to advance the government of God. King Herod tried to kill the increase (offspring; Jesus) because he feared the government of God would make man's government obsolete. If Herod could have located the address of Jesus' headquarters, he would have sent all available armies to destroy it. The location of this government will not be identified by an earthly address but by those who embrace Jesus as King of Kings and Lord of Lords in their heart. The invisible kingdom of God within the believer will become visible and obvious through the manifestation of the sons of God!

"Jesus Christ is Lord" becomes the motto, and the cross of Calvary becomes the coat of arms for those who put Jesus on the throne of their heart. He rules and reigns from an auspicious address deep down in my heart. This strange location gives Jesus a place from which to increase kingdom rule and gives me a place from which to decrease selfish desires. We should evaluate where we are in this process as compared to where He wants us to be. Is He on the throne in my life? Am I fulfilling my predetermined destiny to advance and increase?

Nearly Knocked Off Our Feet

I don't suppose I will ever forget the struggle to sort out all the different emotions that come from the kind of report we had just received. From fear to anger . . . from intermittent peace to confusion . . . from keen love for my wife to despair as I thought of what she might have to face: I went through all of these thoughts and feelings in a matter of minutes. I know she did, too. Our faith would surge to the surface and temporarily hold us steady until the next sentence came from the doctor's mouth. Then the emotional cycle would start over again as we went through a consultation that seemed to suspend time.

I didn't tell Tami, but I suspected something grim by the tone of concern in the nurse's voice as she asked us to come in to visit with the doctor. "Please be seated, I'm afraid I've got some unfortunate news," were the words that confirmed what I had been feeling. At that point the emotional roller coaster was well underway. The report that followed just accelerated the speed of the ride. "There are four classes of thyroid cancer—class one the most desirable and class four the worst. Tami, according to the biopsies and the cultures, you have class four."

This was 1985, and we had been in full time ministry for five years, traveling as itinerant evangelists. The ministry base and financial foundation had been carefully built and it appeared to be on solid footing. But it is interesting how one report can shake your foundation and rock your world. Many of my readers understand all too well what I am saying. The results of one phone call can alter every activity or thought; one day can rearrange the rest of your life.

But I thought these types of things were not supposed to happen to us. After all, we had given up all to "answer the call."

As ministers sold out for the work of God, I believed that the surefootedness, direction and mobility of our ministry had been established on the will of God. Our spiritual feet had been shod with the preparation of the gospel of peace, and we were advancing, to the best of our ability, by putting our feet down on the head of Satan.

The fact that we had unreservedly given ourselves to the work of God brought stability on one hand. But on the other, because I felt like the Lord had forsaken me, my foundation seemed very unstable. My stable scriptural underpinnings that had kept me prepared for any battle with the enemy was now shaken to the core. After I had given up a career in the family business to be obedient to a call of God, how could the Lord let this happen? What had we overlooked or neglected; what had we done to receive this judgment? How could I continue to preach about healing when my wife was dealing with cancer in her throat? Maybe we should postpone surgery and wait on God.

These and other troubling questions continued to flood my spirit like a steady stream splashing down a mountainside, yet we followed the advice of the doctors and scheduled surgery. I thought I had sufficiently used the gospel of peace to prepare my spiritual equilibrium for seasons like this, but until we empty ourselves of pride by admitting weakness, God's hands are tied. He won't fill something that we don't empty. I was weak and I admitted it. In the midst of our problems, my personal prayer vigils became some of the most memorable to date. Although the questions remained, I learned to cherish the simple things of life . . . the love of the Lord and my wife. From nowhere, faith seemed to gush into me like a river.

Although Tami could not travel with me as much, the meetings I conducted were especially anointed. The increase of the favor of God came in direct proportion to the amount of my "decreasing." The more I emptied, the more God filled. Never have I enjoyed Jesus like I did during this season. It was special.

But watching my darling wife fight cancer wasn't special. It was painful. Maybe you have witnessed the effects of disease in the body of a loved one. With every passing day your love and empathy increase, until you wish you could take their place. The depth of my pain was commensurate with the depth of my love.

This reminds me of Jesus (not that I should be compared to our Savior). The joy and pain of the cross, because of Jesus' love for us, is well documented in the Bible. His pain was not just a physical pain, but also a brokenheartedness because of our sinful plight. His joy was because of the new spiritual possibilities that His blood would bring.

If the gospel of peace is a viable part of our spiritual armor, it must bring peace. Remember, the soldier from Ephesians had his feet shod with the gospel of peace. It truly was amazing how armed we felt with the peace of God during this entire ordeal. Peace (gospel of peace) as armor truly gave us the firm footing and understanding during this storm, and gave us hope of once again advancing.

From all reports, Tami underwent successful surgery to remove her thyroid and parathyroids. Further biopsies were taken to confirm all cancer was removed and she spent three days in isolation while they administered radioactive iodine as a precautionary measure in the event some cancer had been overlooked during surgery.

Post-surgical checkups appeared to be routine—until further tests revealed more cancer in her throat. Apparently, the surgeon and the radiation treatments had missed some cancerous tumors. We went from the doctor's office, reeling from that report, directly to the hospital to say an eternal goodbye to Tami's dying grandmother. It was too late. Grandma Liford didn't wait for us to get there. Talk about tough days. Talk about shaking your foundation.

Life experiences challenge our physical strength and emotional stability. Spiritual surefootedness is also tested during days like the one I am describing. If you have adequately prepared your foundation or surefootedness through the gospel of peace, trial and testing will declare it to be so. To successfully battle like a spiritual soldier against physical cancer, and battle for spiritual equilibrium, one must have on the proper armor.

And in this case, having our feet shod with the gospel of peace prepared us for round two of this fight against cancer. The only thing I knew to do, I did . . . pray, pray, pray. But the more I prayed, the more upset I became. I was upset with God for allowing this long, drawn-out ordeal and mad at the devil for his incessant attacks. These were intense spiritual and emotional times, but righteous resolve declared victory over the enemy of cancer.

Not long after grandma's funeral, and as we were trying to decide the best defense against this newly discovered cancer, we went to our home church in Indianapolis, Indiana, to hear Evangelist Lloyd Bustard speak. As he was walking down the aisle during a time of ministry, he said, "If anyone in this section has cancer, stand in the aisle, because God wants to heal you." At that time, Lloyd did not know us nor we him, but the Lord knew us both. The prayer was special, though in some ways routine, because Tami didn't feel any change or surge. But we went from that prayer for Tami to a very exciting report from the latest biopsy.

Tami was mysteriously cancer-free. The post-surgical discovery of cancer was gone. We knew something the medical profession did not know; we could explain something they could not. Tami was healed through the obedience of an evangelist, through the power of the blood of Jesus, and because of her faith in the finished work of the cross!

The only plausible medical explanation was that the radioactive iodine finally found its designated target. However, we knew that the prayer of healing had hit its target. We had stood, sometimes shaky but stood nonetheless, as warriors whose feet were shod with the gospel of peace. The firm foundation available to every spiritual soldier kept us surefooted yet, at the same time, mobile enough to advance. We were then poised and readied to continue conquering new spiritual territory by putting our feet down on the head of our enemy. This cancer ordeal may have bruised our spiritual heel but it crushed the enemy's head. Tami has been cancer free ever since!

LOCATION IS NOT A GEOGRAPHY QUESTION

When, in the earthly utopia, sin contaminated the call of God on Adam and Eve, the fall of man resulted; but the call of God is higher than the fall of man. The charge to keep the garden was the call of administration and stewardship. The voice of God came to Adam to inquire of him concerning his proximity to the call. The Lord God called and asked, "Where art thou?" (see Genesis 3:9)

> The rhetorical question, "Where art thou?" was designed to show Adam where he was in relationship to where he was supposed to be. When Adam came clean, it revealed his spiritual position, not his physical location.

The Lord was not inquiring because He could not locate Adam. Be assured that the Creator knew the whereabouts of His creation. This rhetorical question was designed to show Adam where he was in relationship to where he was supposed to be. When Adam came clean, it revealed his spiritual position, not his physical location. We would do well to allow the Almighty to ask us the same.

Where are we in comparison to the Lord's predetermined purposes for our lives? Can you pinpoint exactly where your call has carried you? Have you followed His plan for your life into deeper revelation, or ignored it because of rebellion? Are you content to be prepared without seeing any real progress?

For some, these probing questions reveal the lack of progress. We have been armed with the call, but certainly have not become dangerous to the devil. Because of our lack of progress, our enemy has considered us a non-threat, but with proper stewardship of our prayer life we can become armed and dangerous. Our feet have not been shod with the gospel of peace so we can flee from the devil, but so we can run toward the battle.

Prayer Principle #3:

Prayer Principle of Right Timing: Deals With Confusion

Sandals are for footing, foundation and direction. When this part of the armor is applied and activated through prayer, proper alignment in the government of God will bring peace, progress, and increase.

Dear Lord,

I pray today to put on the armor necessary for the spiritual struggle around me. I must be well equipped because the enemy is always on the offensive. By faith, I put the necessary military equipment on my feet. I pray to put peace on my feet as a foundational part of the gospel.

May my feet be shod with the preparation of the gospel of peace according to Ephesians 6:17. The world is full of fear and confusion, but I dress my feet with the gospel of peace.

Like Your Word declares, let peace rule my heart. May Your peace prepare me with every scriptural and spiritual footing. I want to be ready to progress for the kingdom of God.

Dear Lord, I thank You for the direction and the mobility that battle-ready footwear gives me. I will go where You want me to go. Thank You for leading and guiding me on my journey. Thank You for applying protection to my foundation. In my spiritual journey, I have a foundation of peace and the solid footing of preparedness.

Now I pray to move from a defensive position to an offensive position. I don't want to stand still, but I desire to progress and advance into the enemy's territory. Help me to tear down the kingdom of the devil and establish the kingdom of God. Of the increase of Your government and of peace, there will be no end.

Thank You for the ability to activate the gospel of peace through this prayer of proper alignment. Line me up, Lord! In every part of my life. Line me up with You and Your Word. I know this prayer for the increase of the government of God will indeed bring peace, firm footing, direction and mobility. Thank You that today I am fulfilling my calling and will progress in the things of God.

In Jesus' name. Amen.

TWO POINT PRAYER PLAN:

1. START PRAYING NOW
2. NEVER STOP PRAYING

— CHAPTER FIVE —

Persuasion Brings Protection

Activating the Fourth Piece of Spiritual Armor Through Prayer

The Shield of Faith

Above all take the shield of faith with which you will be able to quench the fiery darts of the wicked one.

Praying always with all prayer.

—Ephesians 6:16, 18

Ephesians 6:16 mentions the fourth piece of armor—the shield of faith. The original language translates *faith* as "persuasion." Persuasion can be very powerful if what one believes causes action, but inaction calls into question the validity of the persuasion. Our creed should establish our deeds, and our belief should determine our behavior.

It has been said that we believe the part of the Bible only to the degree that we act upon it. Generally, *to persuade* is defined as "to cause to believe in" and *persuasion* means "to act according to that belief." It's easy to see how closely related these two concepts are. To act according to a deep and conscious conviction always brings results. Trouble will always be the outcome if one's scriptural belief does not result in improved spiritual behavior, but persuasion brings protection. We must hear and do the Word of God we've been given as opposed to a preoccupation with searching for a fresh or different word.

> Our creed should establish our deeds, and our belief should determine our behavior.

Prior to Moses' "changing of the guard" ceremony, which he conducted so the people would accept Joshua's leadership and go into the Promised Land, he challenged them with an interesting instruction. From his leadership perspective the children of Israel were making the Word of God too mysterious and far off. He said they should not send emissaries to heaven for a different word or send out a search team across the seas to bring home a word that they could hear and do. They already had the word from Moses (see Deuteronomy 30:14). The only missing component was obedience to it . . . sound familiar?

This advice pertains to all occasions but especially during times of transition similar to the setting found here. When a church, movement or ministry undergoes transition, the emphasis should be the same as it was for the children of Israel . . . do the word already in your heart and mouth. In order to move from slavery to freedom, we must be persuaded enough to act on what we already know.

If, as suggested by the definition, persuasion brings action, why are so many Christians who claim to be full of faith so inactive? Is it not time to apply and activate the armor and become more militarily minded concerning the advancement of the kingdom of God? In order to take any new territory, we need to launch a fresh, bold, and innovative offensive into the kingdom of darkness. Without faith as a shield, we limit our capabilities and tie the hands of God. Remember, Paul said, "Above all, take up the shield of faith."

THE STORES OR THE CHORES

In the 1965 television series, Green Acres, Oliver Wendell Douglas found himself fired from a distinguished New York law firm for growing mushrooms in his desk drawer, so he began growing crops on the terrace of his Park Avenue penthouse. While on a business trip to Chicago one weekend, he bought the old Haney place in Hooterville (just take the train—the Cannonball—out from Pixley). In his new role as proprietor of the "prestigious" Haney farm, Oliver was occupied with unending chores; but because of his inexperience and a lot of bad advice, he had trouble completing most basic farm assignments. Yet, he loved his new occupation.

Lisa Douglas, Oliver's fussy wife, on the other hand, thought farm living was no life at all. Being a high society sophisticate from New York City, she was devastated to find out that Hooterville had no beauty salons or specialty shops. Lisa wanted "Times Square" while Oliver longed for "fresh air." Every time she suggested "the stores," he countered with "the chores." She wanted the stores of New York instead of the chores of farm life. This philosophical difference surfaced constantly and inspired many enjoyable episodes.

Oliver's conviction and persuasion as to the definition of a fulfilling life pulled him, like a giant magnet, away from the opulence of the city and into the rigorous duties of farm life. Although Lisa preferred they do something other than farming, Oliver, a typical entrepreneur, assumed the risk of "farming for a living." This should be the attitude of every Christian who says they are serious about fighting the good fight by using the shield of faith. Remember, faith means persuasion, and persuasion is defined as acting according to belief. When you truly live by faith, you can "make a living" at it.

Spiritual riches might give you the wherewithal to shop the stores, but someone must break the mall mentality in the modern church and do some chores. There are plenty of positions available in the kingdom of God, and we must work while it is day—for when night falls, the work stops. We must act. *If somebody doesn't stay home and do the chores, one day there will be no money to shop the stores.*

Because of the continual deterioration of the Christian work ethic, we are in jeopardy of losing our purchasing power until we can only afford to window-shop. We cannot afford to rest in the exceeding riches of God's grace without acting responsibly. It is time to roll up our spiritual sleeves and get some chores done. "Pray for laborers for the harvest" is the inspired instruction of Jesus (see Matthew 9:30). His words suggest that the labor problem could be corrected if believers were employed in prayer.

Do or Be Deceived

The pastoral counsel of James, the brother of Jesus, to the Jerusalem church reminds us that talk is cheap. In his letter, he instructed the believers not to be hearers of the word of the Lord only, but doers also. He plainly explains how people can deceive themselves (see James 1:22, 25).

These verses declare that unless we do something with what we have heard, we are actually agents of our own deception. The devil gets a lot of undeserved credit for deceiving us. And other times friends and family get blamed, but truly we deceive ourselves by simply "not doing." We not only have the potential to be the agent of our own deception, but we can also be the agent of our own blessing.

We all get upset when we realize we've been scammed or deceived. However, what about when we scam ourselves out of a blessing? Who do we accuse in this blame game? Remember James promised: *"a doer will be blessed in what he does."* The blessing comes by "doing" and the deception comes by "not doing."

Faith Activated by Actions

Faith without works cannot really be called faith. The draw and demand placed on our faith only comes through action. Actions make faith work and, until we act, our faith remains dead. Faith works only when it is worked; and for it to truly be considered faith, it must produce a deed and be evidenced by the doing. More than words (verbal faith) and more than mere knowledge (mental faith), true faith must be active and visible. Real faith inspires action, manifests itself in works, and is demonstrated by obedience. James 2:17, 20, and 26 declare that faith without works is dead, alone and useless.

If the activation of our faith requires action, what must we do? What work must be done in order to energize our spiritual existence? Scripture reveals the simple solution to maintaining the delicate balance of faith and works. All works with no faith is legalism; but all faith and no works is impossible, because it would be dead; therefore, maintaining a proper combination between creed and deed, between faith and works is the key. In prayer we must leave room for a rhema word from God, because faith comes by hearing and hearing comes from a (rhema) word (see Romans 10:17). Prayer is a tremendous way to activate our protective shield of faith. Prayer should be a two-way street, with both parties taking turns talking and listening. When we listen, rhema words come and faith is established. Prayer builds faith. The book of Hebrews perfectly connects faith and prayer (see Hebrews 11:6).

Here we find the recommendation to the spiritual soldier for what is necessary to quench the assignment of the enemy sent to assail him. This passage also tells us how to please God . . . use faith. A spiritual struggle is no different than many military campaigns fought in the natural. The one receiving directives must believe in the one giving the directives. We must believe that God is; and that He is the Captain of our salvation, issuing orders that we can trust. When we have this level of faith, it pleases God and He rewards our requests. Jude 20 reports that prayer can accomplish the building of our faith. This passage propounds that we build our spiritual house and advance faith by prayer.

Faith and Prayer

A desire for the Lord will compel us to pray. If prayer is based in anything other than a deep desire to be in the presence of the Lord, it stops short of a faith-filled prayer and becomes obligation or duty. Too often, prayer has been reduced to an escape from problems or an attempt at an immediate relief of pressure. We don't need jailhouse Christianity that goes like this: "I got God because I got in trouble."

> Too often, prayer has been reduced to an escape from problems or an attempt at an immediate relief of pressure.

As believers, we should not have the same jailhouse mentality when it comes to prayer. We should not just pray to relieve the pressure of a situation, but to develop a loving relationship with the Lord which compels us into a perpetual appetite for more of Jesus. The book of Proverbs warns against having an appetite for the delicacies of the world, for they are deceptive. We must hunger for the nourishment found only in Jesus. I love the word *diligently* found in Hebrews 11:6. It means "crave," "search out," or "to investigate thoroughly." This combustible hunger combined with faith explodes in the heart of God until He rewards our request.

The combination of hunger-driven prayer and faith is found throughout the Scripture; however, it has particular emphasis in the New Testament.

> *The prayer of faith shall save the sick.* —James 5:14

> *Therefore I say unto you, what things you desire, when you pray, believe that you receive them, and you shall have them.* —Mark 11:24

> *Jesus answered and said unto them, Assuredly, I say unto you If you have faith and do not doubt you will not only do what I have done to the fig tree but also if you say to this mountain Be removed and be cast into the sea it will be done. And whatever things, you ask in prayer, believing, you will receive.* —Matthew 21:21–22
>
> *So Jesus said to them, Because of your unbelief for assuredly I say to you if you have faith as a mustard seed you shall say to this mountain Move from here to there and it will move and nothing will be impossible for you.*
> —Matthew 17:20
>
> *But let him ask in faith with no doubting for he who doubts is like a wave of the sea driven and tossed by the wind.* —James 1:6

These and other passages illustrate how prayer can help activate faith. Until we become more aggressive in prayer, we might be recognized as spiritual soldiers but seldom be rewarded with the advancement of our offensive objectives. *Prayer changes a soldier from "armed but not dangerous" to "armed and dangerous."* It moves him from the defensive-minded survivor to an offensive threat. Prayer helps activate the shield of faith until no part of the person is unprotected. Persuasion brings protection. What are you really persuaded by? What do you truly care about? What consumes your thoughts, dreams, and desires? Protection comes by standing strong for your convictions, beliefs, and persuasions.

> This combustible hunger combined with faith explodes in the heart of God until He rewards our request.

JESUS PRAYS FOR PETER'S PERSUASION

Why are we dictated by the desires of our carnal nature? To rise above the whims and wishes of the flesh is a lifelong battle, and as Peter illustrates, our closeness to the Lord does not ensure victory over our fallen nature and its influence. Presumably, the disciples should have been able to successfully stand when doubt and denial came calling; however, this was not the case. Simon Peter caved in when the carnal nature challenged him, and he eventually denied three times that he ever knew the Lord.

Jesus knew Peter's faith was going to be tested through the struggle between Satan's desire to sift him and his desire to remain loyal to the Lord. Sifting originates in a practice of the oriental farmer who would measure the wind to calculate the weight of the seed against the strength of the wind. Because the chaff grew along with the wheat, upon harvesting the farmer would sift the harvest to separate them. If the wind was too light, the chaff, which was lighter than wheat, would not blow away. If the wind was too strong, the wheat and the chaff would blow away and both would be lost. The good and the bad can grow together just like Peter and Judas coexisted for 3½ years, but when the wind blows the sifting process should reveal the chaff and purge it from the good. Simply stated: Satan wanted to blow Peter away. But because of Jesus' prayer, Peter was "heavy" enough to stay in the harvest. When Jesus told Peter about this request of the enemy to sift and shake him, Jesus said parenthetically, "I've made you a request of mine." The thought that Jesus prayed for Peter during this temptation of the enemy must have relieved some of his potential anxiety (see Luke 22:31–32).

The impending battle would take its toll on Peter, and Jesus knew it. Jesus offers something better than counsel or instruction—He prayed for Peter. He knew this was the only option to enhance Simon Peter's spiritual survival. Moreover, it wasn't just a general prayer of blessing or support. It wasn't a prayer for escape (Jesus knew Simon needed to go through this process). It was a prayer for Simon's faith to withstand the wind during the sifting process. Jesus knew that if that faith failed, it would preclude a return to the Lord and restrict the will of God for him.

The topic of Jesus' prayer is worthy of further discussion. He did not pray for Simon Peter's attitude, endurance, or abilities. Jesus did not pray for Peter's physical, emotional, or financial well-being. He prayed for Peter's faith. Jesus understood the most important thing he could pray for was the faith of Peter. This vividly underscores the connection between prayer and faith.

Faith makes recovery possible, and in addition it promotes restoration. That's why Jesus prayed for Peter's faith first. Jesus used this prayer for faith as a weapon to withstand Satan, and He does the same thing for you and me. An investigation into the post ascension activities of Jesus reveals His heart for us. Even now He can be found praying for us before the throne, using the ministry of intercession (see Romans 8:43; Hebrews 7:25).

Sifting and Separation

When Satan desired to sift Simon, he was only trying to pervert a godly process proclaimed by John the Baptist when he was preaching about the coming of his cousin, Jesus. John said Jesus would come like a winnowing fan and sift the good from the bad. The devil always tries to steal righteous concepts and corrupt godly methods. John the Baptist prepared the way for Jesus through his preaching, he rebuked the religious leaders by calling them a brood of vipers and he preached repentance to them. Jesus used the same title for the Pharisees. Also, in the third chapter of Matthew, John drew a distinction between the baptism of repentance and the baptism of the Holy Spirit by making a reference to the original God-ordained purpose for sifting.

> The original design of sifting was to separate the good from the bad, not the good from the good. Always remember: if the sifting or separation tears good away from good, it is not God.

Satan's sifting was a perversion of that pure process because he tried to separate Simon from Jesus. The original design of sifting was to separate the good from the bad, not the good from the good. Always remember: if the sifting or separation tears good away from good, it is not God. Here John declares the purpose of sifting, to be conducted through the Holy Spirit, to be a personal purging where the wheat and chaff inside one's soul could be separated.

We have relegated the Matthew 3:12 verse to the final judgment, but the idea within the context of John's sermon regarding two separate fires has been overlooked. Listen to Eugene Peterson's *The Message Bible:*

> *I'm baptizing you here in the river, turning your old life in for a kingdom life. The real action comes next: The main character in this drama—compared to him I'm a mere stagehand—will ignite the kingdom life with you, a fire within you, the Holy Spirit within you, changing you from the inside out. He's going to clean house—make a clean sweep of your lives. He'll place everything true in its proper place before God; everything false he'll put out with the trash to be burned.*

The first half of verse 12 better relates to the process of sifting through the Spirit as listed in verse 11 than it does the eternal fire. Let me explain.

There are two fires: the Holy Ghost fire and the eternal judgment fire. The first fire (Holy Spirit baptism) sifts and separates, and the second fire burns what was separated. The first fire, Holy Spirit baptism, is the "winnowing" fan that blows the chaff, separating it from the wheat so it can be burned. The unquenchable fire of judgment can only be applied after the sifting has separated the bad from the good. Judgment (fire) comes after separation (sifting). The Holy Spirit does the sifting.

The second chapter of Acts underscores the Spirit's involvement in the sifting process. The baptism of fire prophesied by John the Baptist, in Matthew chapter three, came to pass in Acts chapter two. What a glorious fire initially fell on 120 believers in the upper room. Just read the story line to see the sifting fan blowing across the lives of this disciple and subsequently on others.

THE DEVIL'S DARTS

Charles Spurgeon wrote, "Every Christian is born a warrior. It is his destiny to be assaulted; it is his duty to attack." The enemy also continually looks for an opportunity to attack us. Because his fiery darts can go undetected, we must always be prepared. A well-prepared warrior stands ready for a sudden and unexpected onslaught. Small firebrands, in ancient warfare, were twisted into the form of arrows or darts and could be shot from a bow or hurled by hand, making the smallest opening in the armor an opportunity for the enemy. These mini-missiles often came without any warning. Many times the success of the dart was due to its suddenness and soundlessness.

This is a perfect picture of the way the devil works his wickedness. His deceptive capabilities must not be under-appreciated; remember, he talked one out of every three angels in heaven into a war against God. This clear picture of deception vividly portrays true satanic desire—total destruction. To perpetrate anguish, turmoil, pain, confusion, frustration, and fear (just to name a few) is his desire for each person alive, believer and non-believer alike. His ultimate dream since the beginning remains physical and spiritual death for everyone. Surprise attacks from small darts of discouragement and division, if left unquenched, can be fatal. We must get ready and stay prepared if we want to stay protected, but we can take encouragement from the promise of Isaiah. This Scripture reassures us that no weapon formed against us will prosper (see Isaiah 54:17).

A good offence includes defense. We should add to our defensive position of protection a strategy to include the offensive. We must not yield to the tyranny of the "either/or" but we are submitting to the blessings of the "both/and." We can be offensive and defensive.

In the book of Galatians, Paul, after addressing the carnal-minded people who were on the defensive because of surrendering to the flesh, turned to the sincere saints and said, "Be not weary in well doing because in due season you will reap if you don't faint" (see Galatians 6:9). The apostle Paul revealed to the Galatians that a satanic attack of weariness can come not only from wrongdoing but from doing right.

We must keep the shield of faith up and stay moving forward by doing well, even when we grow weary. Accordingly, weariness is no excuse for not doing well.

Our Opportunistic Enemy

James 4:7 reminds us to resist the devil and he will flee from us. The word *resist* suggests "standing against" or "opposing in a militaristic sense." This conveys the picture of a soldier who, when under attack, defends himself. We know for a fact that when we do resist Satan, he will return. He will come back to take advantage of any weakness, so we must always be ready to defend ourselves from future attacks.

Jesus warned that as soon as a demonic spirit leaves a man it begins looking for the opportune time to return to the house (physical body) from which it was cast. It is possible for people to inadvertently give place to the devil by not filling up the house with the Holy Spirit in place of a wicked spirit, and by not replacing the lies of Satan with the Word of God.

The unique timing of our enemy is calculated and directed. He loves to attack us on our turf when we least expect it. When we should be enjoying God's presence, celebrating victories or ministering to others, often a sense of impending spiritual attack from the devil torments us. He ruthlessly attacks us in our church or during active days of healthy ministry. We need to be ready when we set aside time for prayer and fasting. Predictably, the devil—cold and calculating—waits in the wings for an opportune time to attack, much like a robber waits in the darkness or like an animal waits to pounce on its prey. The devil knows when not to spring, but he also knows when to spring—when we least expect it. David did not expect to see Bathsheba bathing as he surveyed the landscape. This was not a coincidence but an opportunistic enemy working his diabolical plan when David least expected it.

Even Jesus was not exempt from such an evil approach. After Jesus' forty days of testing, the devil departed from Him for a period, but the text suggests Satan used a temporary retreat to wait for a weakness, hoping to resume the assault. Listen to the language recorded in Luke 4:13.

And when the devil had ended all the temptation, he departed from Him (Jesus) until an opportune time. —*Luke 4:13*

Jesus later shared with us the victorious outcome over this opportunistic enemy. The Scripture reports that when Satan tried to return, he found no place in the Lord. We must stay on guard and full of the Spirit and the Word of God.

Miracles transpire when a *kairos* time and a *chronos* time intersect. *Kairos* time is an appointed time or special season—a time when a divine dispensation overlays ordinary events. *Chronos* is a calendar time. The adversary thought he had judged correctly the vulnerability of Jesus when, in three separate attempts, he tempted and tested Jesus' resolve, only to resign himself to return to Jesus at a future *kairos*.

The word "opportune" in Luke 4:13 is the Greek word *kairos*. The devilish desire is an evil use of a *kairos* time in your life, ministry, family, or church. Our opportunistic enemy lurks and lingers around the edges of your life, trying to correctly time an evil opportunity.

> You must not criticize what you permit and you cannot condemn what you allow!

Also notice the root word *port* from which we build the word *opportunity*. Obviously, a port represents a door, gateway, or entrance. The word *import* also derives from the original word *port*. We must not give the devil any entrance, door, or opportunity where he can import pain, heartache, confusion, or fear. You must not criticize what you permit and you cannot condemn what you allow! Paul specifically supports this idea by using this advice, "We must not give place to the devil" (Ephesians 4:27). When checking the footnote attached to the word "place" in this verse, the word "opportunity" is referred to. "Do not give an opportunity to the devil" is a better translation for this verse. Remember, this is the admonition of the apostle Paul to the believers in Asia. I believe it is also sound spiritual advice for today, for any entrance is a port through which he can gain access into our hearts. I wonder what port of entry Judas gave the devil thereby allowing him access? (see John 13:27)

Faith as a Shield

Paul assigned a position of significance and importance to the shield of faith when he designated it to be "above all." Remember, Hebrews said without faith it is impossible to please God. Whatever other parts of armor may be neglected—the shield must not be forgotten. The girdle, the breastplate, the sandals, the helmet, and the sword should never be neglected, but the shield must be employed above all of these. A shield, being used by a well-trained soldier, could compensate for the loss of all the other parts of a warrior's weaponry.

Because of the mobility of the shield, the soldier using it had a tremendous advantage. Unlike other armor apparatus, the shield always remained unfastened, free from the other pieces. Because of being held on the arm, it could interpose resistance and protection for any unprotected part of a soldier. The style of combat determined the size of the shield, and some shields were large enough to hide the entire body. This familiar cry of Spartan mothers could often be heard when sending sons to war: "Come home dead upon thy shield rather than come home without it." The shield of a foot soldier, large enough to carry a body, had the inscription of the coat of arms, something every soldier prided himself in retaining to the last. The shield's design offered protection to the soldier as well as to other parts of the armor. Although a good shield was indestructible, incombustible, and impenetrable, its effectiveness was predicated upon the person employing it. We really are responsible.

These practical descriptions of an ancient warrior easily parallel those of a spiritual soldier. Faith must be given preeminence as the most important piece of our armor. Above all, we must use faith as a shield, for it can compensate for so many spiritual shortcomings. Faith should be supple, flexible in every confrontation, and adaptable to any enemy engagement. Whatever the size of our spiritual battle, the size of our faith can be commensurate. Faith will always be big enough to offer full protection for the person in battle and protect other parts of the armor. Genuine faith will cover you completely. Faith is indestructible; it can never be destroyed. Faith is incombustible; it can take the heat of any fiery dart. It is impenetrable; nothing can break its protective power.

Most of all, our faith shield bears a Christian coat of arms. Etched on every faith-filled believer's heart should be a cross, our symbol of victory and our family identity. It represents our current glory, and it speaks of our potential gain. The cross of Calvary is the emblem of our conquering King, who has already secured for us the ultimate victory over the enemy of our soul. Faith in the finished work of Calvary so inspires us that we can launch a bold new offensive into the devil's domain.

Our Duty to Attack

Spurgeon said that being assaulted is our destiny. I have witnessed some weary Christian soldiers who have resigned themselves to a life filled only with defending ground previously gained. Being assaulted may be our destiny, but our duty is to attack. An obvious observation from the picture of our warrior and his weapon suggests that the shield is of little use unless handled efficiently in battle. A shield needs to be employed and implemented in order to be effective; when properly used, faith becomes a battering ram to run through any enemy embankments or barricades. As the soldier moved from one enemy to the next during a battle, the shield protected him while he advanced and attacked. This illustrates the best and most productive use of faith. Battle-worthy warriors can use faith as a weapon to recapture ground and to push back the opposition.

Prayer helps apply and fully activate the shield of faith until its use becomes effective offensively and defensively. It can be used for protection while under attack from the enemy and for power while attacking the enemy. A shield fully employed can repel the incoming missiles and, at the same time, allow the soldier to move about and advance. The shield of our persuasion truly does provide protection. Our armor can really be activated to the point where we become *armed and dangerous*.

Prayer Principle #4:

Prayer Principle of Persuasion: Deals with the Opportunistic Enemy

The shield of faith represents the protection from the darts of the devil. This protection comes by becoming a doer and not just a hearer of the Word. You can use faith for defending yourself while simultaneously attacking the enemy. Faith is persuasion, and persuasion inspires action. This prayer restores your faith and inspires action by destroying discouragement.

Our dear heavenly Father,

I pick up my shield by virtue of this prayer. You have designed my spiritual armor for utmost protection. Even if other pieces of armor are inactive, You told me to use this shield above all.

The devil waits for an opportune time to attack, but my shield will be ready. I get dressed today to do battle. I will use my shield of faith, and I will prevail through persuasion. I know faith without works is dead. I also know faith is persuasion and persuasion inspires action. So today, Lord, help me to act.

May my persuasion provoke deeds and my belief demand behavior. I will no longer offer lip service. I give You my life by doing something with what I know. I am activated and energized into an offensive position through powerful persuasion!

By this prayer, may my persuasion prevail as I launch an attack into the kingdom of darkness. The flexible, mobile shield of persuasion will not fail in conflict. Thank You, in Jesus' name, for victory. Amen.

Two point prayer plan:

1. Start praying now
2. Never stop praying

— CHAPTER SIX —

PROTECTED AND PROFOUND

ACTIVATING THE FIFTH PIECE OF SPIRITUAL ARMOR THROUGH PRAYER

THE HELMET OF SALVATION
And take the helmet of salvation . . .
Pray always with all prayer and supplication.
—Ephesians 6:17, 18

WHERE IS THE WISDOM?

While in spiritual conflict, we must protect the place from which flows reasoning and revelation. We must cover the head if we expect to survive and advance in this war. The devil desires to destroy our ability to think, reason, or logically deduce, and he works overtime to dilute our understanding, subvert our wisdom, and destroy revelation. Ephesians lists the fifth piece of armor as the helmet of salvation. Necessary protection afforded to spiritual soldiers comes from the helmet. We must protect our minds from every evil assault while simultaneously protecting ourselves for profound spiritual revelation. Paul said we could have the mind of Christ. Can there be any more profound spiritual thinking than that? We can think like Jesus thought—even in the area of sin and repentance. God-like sorrow should work repentance in us when we think about sin the same way Jesus thought regarding sin. To agree with God in matters of repentance illustrates one of many possibilities for letting the mind of Christ come to our mind.

The Lord dispenses distilled wisdom as we ask for it. If at any point you feel depleted of wisdom, it is available upon request (see James 1:5).

If a simple prayer request would release wisdom, why don't we see more of it working in our lives? The answer is obvious: we have not asked for it. Scripture tells us we have not because we ask not. What don't we have? We don't have what we haven't asked for. The shortage is not because of lack of supply, but lack of demand. If we demand (ask), He will supply. We must not have asked for wisdom, because it doesn't appear to be in abundance. Paul said our Savior is "capable of doing more than what we ask or think" (see Ephesians 3:20). Our profound, inspired thinking and our prayerful asking releases God to act according to the power (power to ask and think) that works in us. The power that works in us is the power of faith to believe that God can do whatever I can think of.

I love the language James uses in this passage as he directs the pastoral oversight of the church at Jerusalem. He gave a promise when he said, "It will be given to him." You and I need to develop a faith-filled dependence upon this word until it brings comfort to us. Our Lord will not withhold wisdom but will liberally release it without reproach, upon request.

What is Wisdom?

Wisdom includes the proper application of knowledge, learning, thinking, logic, understanding, prudence, judgment, and skill. In all of these aspects, wisdom must be applied correctly to truly have wisdom. When Adam and Eve were offered wisdom by the serpent (see Genesis 3:6), they should have applied these aspects. With proper use of all facets of Adam and Eve's reasoning capabilities, they would have realized their God-likeness had already been established. They were created in the image and the likeness of God, thereby already possessing the attribute of wisdom. They sure could have used a revelation of this concept.

When, in disobedience, they ate of the "tree of the knowledge of good and evil," the knowledge of good and evil may have come, but wisdom did not. Now Adam and Eve would have the knowledge of the pain that came from being excommunicated from the Garden of Eden. Later they would have the knowledge of brokenheartedness that came when they buried one son because of being murdered by their other son. They received knowledge of a pain that God never wanted them to know. Knowledge does not guarantee wisdom, but wisdom always shows the proper use of knowledge. Adam and Eve's decision to eat the forbidden fruit shows us that disobeying and mistrusting God is never wise.

Until sin entered the Garden of Eden, Adam and Eve lived in a pleasant, climate-controlled paradise where the lion laid down with the lamb and the fruit fell off the tree in your hand. The path of their life was smooth and straight—not many rocks or curves. However, when they operated under their own understanding, smooth became rough and the straight became a twisted track of unpleasant turns and curves.

The book of Proverbs reminds us how this spiritual journey can be pleasant again, simply by trusting in the Lord:

Lean not on your own understanding but in all of your ways acknowledge Him and He will direct your path. —*Proverbs 3:5*

The word "direct" in this passage means to make smooth and straight. Trusting the understanding of the natural man will make the way much more difficult. If your journey is unbearably difficult, trusting in and leaning on the wisdom of God is the best way to ensure a smooth and straight pathway.

The Oldest Trick in the Book

The helmet of salvation will protect your mind from the lies of the enemy. He has successfully used lies since the Garden of Eden to destroy the purposes of God in our lives. Adam and Eve listened to the lie in the midst of the provision of God's paradise as recounted in the first book of the Bible. The enemy knows we are vulnerable to his deception and subversion even in the middle of Bible-based, Spirit-filled, overcoming lives. Scripture calls him the father of lies—the originator.

The language of Ephesians makes it clear that the devil does not always attack through the obvious and predictable, but his "head on" (on the head) attacks come by way of crafty and cunning strategies called lies. We would be wise not to be deceived by this tactic and not fall for the oldest trick in the book. The oldest trick in the book truly is a lie that manipulates humankind into believing that God restricts and forbids certain things because of a lack of love. If the enemy can get us to mistrust the heart of God and His provision toward us, he will succeed in outwitting us.

Oh, how we need wisdom! Oh, how we need the protection of the helmet of salvation!

Double-mindedness and Doubt

The tendency for double-mindedness represents a very real spiritual problem ... doubt. Double-mindedness is a significant weapon of the enemy from which we need protection. How can this be accomplished?

In the opening comments of the letter James sent to the church of Jerusalem, he addresses how the helmet of salvation can help protect us from the futility of double-mindedness (see James 1:6–8).

Although they sometimes don't recognize it, pastors and church leaders see double-mindedness displayed all the time. Often it is indistinguishable, mislabeled or ignored altogether. What often looks like a lack of commitment or follow-through is actually double-mindedness because of doubt. When people start, then stop; become red hot, then ice cold; move from one ministry to another, or from church to church; or when people are seemingly excited about involvement in a particular area one day but conspicuously missing the next day, it may not merely be a lack of focus or lack of commitment, but quite possibly double-mindedness.

> What often looks like a lack of commitment or follow-through is actually double-mindedness because of doubt.

Often we dismiss the uncommitted as hopeless—perpetual violators unable to break out of an unproductive pattern. Examples abound of people who just can't seem to make any lasting changes. When a person feels scattered, unable to stay focused on one objective, he/she will seldom know the feeling of fulfillment that comes through accomplishment. They are double-minded!

Often we have been told to "make up our minds," but how can this be done? By learning to become single-minded. When single-minded mentality becomes a priority, continuity can come naturally and spontaneously. This may not be so easily accomplished, but it certainly is possible and quite necessary. To win the war over instability, double-mindedness and doubt must be conquered by the armor of the helmet of salvation. Remember, instability starts in the mind when one doubts God's love and concern. The helmet of salvation stabilizes thoughts, promotes correct thinking, encourages sound-mindedness, and protects against unhealthy thinking patterns that promote double-mindedness.

Remember: a double-minded man is unstable in all his ways. The devil will not stop until a total breakdown of stability occurs in every area of your life and he accomplishes his obvious objective. His relentless approach shows no mercy on your thought life, financial stability, emotional makeup, or even your physical soundness. Don't let him start with even a small breakdown of single-mindedness because comprehensive instability, his ultimate goal, starts with seemingly insignificant areas.

Paul said it is possible to have the mind of Christ. We must wear the protective headgear of the helmet of salvation in order to promote single-mindedness and help conquer instability.

Stable Salvation

One of the clearest pictures of single-mindedness found in Scripture comes from our Lord and Savior. He, with unflinching resolve and unbroken focus, looked toward Calvary. Jesus had one thing on His mind—our salvation. Faith in His loving resolve can bring us single-minded assurance.

Our salvation was secured by the work of Jesus on the cross, and our faith in the finished work of Jesus brings secure thoughts, thereby stabilizing our hearts and minds. We need to be constantly reassured of His love. The determination of Jesus to reconcile us to God affords us the privilege of the protective covering of the helmet of salvation. When we stay single-minded, this protective covering brings security.

The Word of God says we can know for certain that our salvation is secure (assurance in our hearts) and this knowing can give us confidence to "ask" and the courage to "do" (see 1 John 3:20–22). Therefore, with the helmet of salvation securely in place, we can pray and become dangerous to the devil because we act and behave according to our beliefs.

The love of God is unconditional, but sometimes my faith in His unconditional love is extremely conditional. Security comes when one can feel safe in the love of God by trusting in the unconditional aspect of it. His love brings my security. When one feels convinced of love, change can come. Love provides the safe surrounding and freedom from fear of rejection. This promotes change. When we feel the stabilizing influence of the love of the Lord, and realize how single-minded He is regarding that love, we are free to transition into single-mindedness. Remember, single-mindedness brings stability. Because He has given us such secure salvation, we can be single-minded and therefore stable in all our ways.

Don't Doubt It

Just like Thomas, who doubted until He became double-minded regarding the resurrection, I watched doubt and double-mindedness debilitate a man I will call Bob. Bob was gifted. His keen mental ability and his inviting personality were not even his best attributes. The most enviable aspect of Bob was his spiritual hunger—not his good looks, quick wit or athletic ability. His heart after God became clear to me some 17 years ago, shortly after I assumed the pastorate of our church in Racine, Wisconsin. No discernment was needed when appraising the obvious display of spiritual hunger working in this man. One quick glance would reveal it. To Bob, the calling of God on his life developed like a Polaroid picture; the longer he looked at it, the clearer it became. Some of us saw it right away. From poise in preaching that belied his years to an ability to inspire people, Bob had it going for him.

Through the years I have tried to determine where things got off track in Bob's life. Family difficulties, negative friends, critical-spirited associates, or lack of trust in leadership may have contributed to his demise—but these things merely represent something much more significant. The real issue was double-mindedness caused by doubt. Double-mindedness is easy to assess. It produces predictably jerky patterns of start-stop, hot-cold and maybe-maybe not. Double-mindedness destroys momentum, confidence and progress. Because of its disruptive nature, double-mindedness dictates the timing, depth and duration of a person's involvement in any, and ultimately every, activity. I witnessed the negative results in Bob's personal life and public ministry, and I grieved.

Pastor James at Jerusalem reveals the chilling result of double-mindedness: "A double-minded man is unstable in all of his ways and let not that man suppose he will receive anything from the Lord." Remember, Satan wants a comprehensive breakdown of stability. If people continually operate from a position of instability because of double-mindedness, spiritual progress will be virtually nonexistent. I witnessed this downward progression in Bob's life as he struggled to maintain stability in all areas. Double-minded instability, the out-working of doubt, brought the most potentially anointed man I have ever known to a complete spiritual standstill.

> If people continually operate from a position of instability because of double-mindedness, spiritual progress will be virtually nonexistent.

The discussion of double-mindedness and instability must not stop short of mentioning doubt. Looking back, this is where Bob struggled the most. He doubted the love of family and friends. Something made him doubt the call and purposes of God on his life. Critical and divisive voices caused him to doubt the sincerity of leadership. He even came to question his own abilities. Unsatisfied with current levels of doubt and double-mindedness in Bob's life, the enemy did not stop. He never will until we wake up the warrior in us and activate the helmet of salvation. Finally, Bob even doubted the Word of God and its basic tenets—like the resurrection. Today he still struggles with doubts regarding a successful return to the plans and purposes of God for his life. He doubts if, and how, that could work. He doubts the ability of the Spirit to restore the years the insects from the enemy have eaten.

In order to conquer the debilitating doubt and double-mindedness that immobilized this man, we must reconsider the equipment supplied to us from our Commander-in-Chief—the Lord Jesus Christ. He has provided the armor needed to survive the battle and win the war. He would not put us in a battle, yet withhold necessary equipment. Prayer can help us apply and activate the helmet of salvation. The assurance of our salvation, inspired by God's love, can provide a hedge of spiritual protection for our head. We must not doubt His love.

If you recognize this pattern of doubt, double-mindedness and instability in your life, please don't ignore it. Don't allow it to continue uninterrupted. If you ignore it, the advantage in this spiritual struggle will be acquiesced to the enemy. Admit double-mindedness and deal with it by praying faith-filled prayers that activate the helmet of salvation. God loves us and wants us safe and successful in spiritual battle. Do not doubt it! He wants us stable in our salvation and advancing against the enemy. Do not doubt it! And He wants the kingdom of God to be established in us and through us. Please, do not doubt it!

WHAT IS SINGLE-MINDEDNESS?

From the book of Matthew, we can learn the definition of single-sightedness, but what is single-mindedness? Are they related one to the other? Can single-sightedness lead to single-mindedness? The concept of single, when considered from Matthew, may add insight (see Matthew 6:22–23).

Good and bad eyesight are contrasted here; "clear" is contrasted to "cloudy," and "healthy" is compared to "unhealthy." In the language of the Living Bible, Matthew 6:23 makes a connection between spiritual sight and our thought life, and between single-mindedness and single-sightedness.

If your eye is clouded with evil thoughts and desires, you are in deep spiritual darkness.

This happened to Adam and Eve in the Garden of Eden. The trees God had created were pleasant to the eyes and good for food (see Genesis 2:9). In other words, they were "easy on the eyes." In Genesis 3:6, we find the connection between sight and thoughts. The serpent was in the midst of this paradise to obscure the true beauty of the trees with a desire for artificial intelligence. He told Adam and Eve they could be wise (see Genesis 3:6).

The word "wise" means to make one circumspect and, hence, intelligent. The serpent was subtle enough to attack the thinking processes of God's creation by double-sightedness and doubt. And the result became obvious when neither Adam nor Eve could stay focused in faith, but doubted God's Word. They vacillated between what the serpent said and what God said.

THE SPIRITUAL HELMET AS A MENTAL HEDGE

God gave Adam specific instructions to keep the Garden of Eden (see Genesis 2:15).

I love the idea conveyed by the word "keep" in this verse. It comes from the Hebrew word *shamar*, meaning to protect by putting a hedge about. Adam failed at his commission to protect the garden by building a hedge around it. When he fell, the Lord God placed cherubims at the end of Eden to "keep" the way of the tree of life (see Genesis 3:24). I find it interesting that, because Adam failed to keep the garden, God had to keep the Tree of Life. This clearly communicates God's desire to keep, hedge, and protect His creation.

If we are to keep our minds and thoughts with single-minded stability, we must do so by using the helmet of salvation prayer from Ephesians 6:17–18 as a hedge of protection. This prayer can serve as a hedge to keep the garden of our mind free from unwanted thistles and uninvited weeds. The first place the serpent gained entrance in the garden was actually in the mind of Eve because she did not properly protect and keep it. If we don't use the helmet of salvation for protection we will, out of our own neglect, allow the serpent to come in and confuse our thoughts and blur our spiritual sight.

> If we don't use the helmet of salvation for protection we will, out of our own neglect, allow the serpent to come in and confuse our thoughts and blur our spiritual sight.

When we use the protective helmet as a hedge of protection, we will be able to live a productive spiritual life with a sense of true peace. The spiritual death that resulted in Adam and Eve will not befall you and me. With a spiritually protected mind, we can be subjected to the "higher law," the law of God (see Romans 8:6–7).

All I See Is Black

All of our children have been subjected to an exercise to expand their imagination and creative thinking skills. Like many parents and teachers, I ask them to close their eyes and go on an imaginary mental trip. After describing a beautiful rolling meadow with a deer drinking water at a bend in a bubbling brook to our daughter when she was four, I asked her if she saw what I was so eloquently describing. "Don't you see the deer drinking water?" I pressed. Her cute response inspired interesting insight. With her eyes scrunched closed, she said, "Dad, all I see is black!"

Pray, put on the helmet of salvation to protect your mind, and you will see with eyes of faith. This will inspire you to stretch into a new place of creativity and spiritual thinking. To establish fresh thought patterns is no easy task. Many times when others see the beauty and serenity of a situation, all you can see is black. We all know that thoughts can either inspire hope and faith, or they can engender hopelessness and fear.

It really is interesting how two people can look at the same situation and have two totally different takes on it. There were two thieves at Calvary equidistant from Jesus yet eternities apart in perspectives. Thus they were eternities apart in their destinies. When looking at Jesus, one saw a criminal and the other saw a Savior. One was saved, the other lost. Perspective is reality. When pondering about how to think, remember the devil always wants you to see black, and the Lord always wants you to see through the light of His love and grace. If thoughts and prayers can stay focused by using the prayer for single-mindedness, stability will be the profound result.

To the church at Philippi, Paul emphasized the importance of employing peace to guard our minds through prayer (see Philippians 4:6–7). As a result, Paul went on to recite the things on which we would be able to meditate. He said to "think on things that were 'true, noble, just, pure, lovely, and of a good report.' "

As illustrated with the other pieces of armor, we can also use prayer to help activate the armor we're wearing. With the helmet of salvation in place for the protection of my mind, and single-minded prayer as the inspiration for profound thinking, I can move from armed and not dangerous to armed and dangerous. We must destroy the doubt that causes double-mindedness so we can advance and become more offensive-minded. For this reason, the armor was issued.

PRAYER PRINCIPLE #5:

Prayer Principle of Focus: Deals With Double-mindedness

The helmet prayer secures a proper approach to thinking and reasoning. The prayer for proper thinking is a simple one that releases God's wisdom and rebukes the devil's lies. This prayer for single-mindedness protects our spiritual nerve center. The devil uses double-mindedness because it brings instability at every level. This prayer approach will encourage stable saints with stable spirits.

Great God of all creation, You alone are worthy to be praised.

You have not left us without the armor we need to prevail in the spiritual struggles of life. Thank You for the way we can be protected by these provisions.

So today, dear Lord, I put on the helmet of salvation to protect my mind, thoughts, reasoning, knowledge and my nerve center—my brain. By faith, I put on the protection needed for the demands of the day. Like a helmet used by athletes for safety and protection, don't let anything damage my head.

Yes, Lord, a protective helmet I put on by virtue of this prayer, and by so doing I pray for single-mindedness. Because double-mindedness brings instability at every level, I activate the armor on my mind by this prayer for single-minded focus.

Lord, I recognize the enemy's attempts to make my mind waver in instability, thereby stripping me of my faith. This is why I pray against double-mindedness. Turn my knowledge into wisdom by making the helmet strong, stable, and powerful. Thank you, dear Lord, for single-mindedness that turns my armor into an active weapon.

Two Point Prayer Plan:

1. Start praying now
2. Never stop praying

— CHAPTER SEVEN —

Success with a Sword

Activating the Sixth Piece of Spiritual Armor Through Prayer

The Sword of the Spirit

The sword of the Spirit which is the Word of God.
Praying always with all prayer and supplication.
—Ephesians 6:17–18

Throughout this work, we have connected prayer and spiritual warfare by emphasizing how prayer helps activate the armor listed in Ephesians 6. The connection between the Word of God as a piece of the armor (verse 17), and prayer (verse 18), illustrates the importance Paul placed on prayer. Ephesians 6:17 lists the sixth piece of spiritual armor as the sword of the Spirit—the Word of God—and verse 18 shows how prayer can also act as a vital weapon when waging warfare against the powers of darkness. After delineating the spiritual armor, he underscored the entire concept by saying: "Pray always using all prayers."

Original Intent Restored Through Prayer and Word

Paul also discussed the combination of prayer and the Word with Timothy, his son in the faith (see 1 Timothy 4:1–5). He instructed Timothy on how to win the war against deceiving spirits and doctrines of demons that pervert the original intent of what God has created. Here the apostle Paul demonstrates the sanctifying power of the Word of God and prayer.

Original intent and purpose can be restored because of prayer and the Word of God. That's what Paul was saying. False teachers and seducing spirits had perverted the pure aspects of marriage and eating by claiming they should be refused and thrown out. We need to remember, God invented eating and marriage for our benefit and pleasure. He did not allow us to enjoy these just so He could turn around and forbid them. The sagacious counsel Paul gives this young pastor is liberating and exciting. The areas being constrained by deceptive doctrines were the very things God created for the believer. That sounds familiar . . . the very things God created for our enjoyment and benefit the devil tries to divert from their original intent and purpose. Even though the devil does not want to see us happy or fulfilled, I've got good news. Prayer and the sword of the Spirit can set us free. The combination of Word (sword of the Spirit) and prayer brings sanctification. When we tackle unclean or defiled situations with the Word, we release what the devil attempts to withhold. Let's use the sword of the Spirit to cut off the

> The very things God created for our enjoyment and benefit the devil tries to divert from their original intent and purpose.

constant flow of spiritual deception that comes from our enemy. This is a part of our armor.

The Word as a Weapon

If we are to stand against the schemes of the devil, we must war with the Word the way Jesus did in the wilderness. He used the "It is written" strategy to war against the enemy, and so should you and I. After every attempt of the enemy to subvert the plan of God, Jesus powerfully and strategically responded with this defense. Remember, the devil tried to persuade Jesus to turn stones to bread. Jesus was the Son of God. He did not have to perform a work to convince Himself and others of who He was. Lingering in His ears were the words from His baptism, "This is My beloved Son in whom I am well pleased."

Jesus refused to reduce His identity to a performance-based system where works would be needed to confirm who He was. He chose to fight with a word He had been previously given. The enemy will eventually depart when confronted with the Word of God. Jesus' war in the wilderness illustrates the promise James gave his Jerusalem church regarding resisting the devil and he will flee (see James 4:7). Hebrews refers to the Word as a weapon in no uncertain terms. The military metaphor is quite revealing (see Hebrews 4:12).

> Jesus refused to reduce His identity to a performance-based system where works would be needed to confirm who He was.

Because God's Word is sharper than a two-edged sword, it can be used as a spiritual weapon with more proficiency than any natural weapon. The sword of the Spirit should always be preferred over man's ability.

Divide and Discern

Success becomes far less elusive when a situation can be "sized up" correctly. Sizing up a situation is simple if it can be broken down into small parts. Parts previously indistinguishable must be divided and separated for better scrutiny and observation. Once the independent value is determined, it becomes easier to appraise the interdependence of each part. The functionality and value of the whole is determined by the dependability and value of each part. God has equipped the spiritual soldier with an uncanny ability to divide and discern.

Have you ever spent too long trying to get a string or rope untangled? How about a fishing line? During spiritual warfare, the enemy skillfully uses his keen ability to confuse everything into one big tangled mess. He wants us to waste a lot of time trying to untangle the mess. He makes things look too complex and complicated by tying everything together like one giant mass of intertwined string.

The first time I met with William, a new believer, I quickly recognized how complicated his life had become. A long trail of abuse from court-appointed guardians, many addictions that had destroyed his health, and possible revocation of his parole represent just a few of the complex situations in the life of this new believer. But the biggest problem he was dealing with was a girlfriend who walked out of his life about the time Jesus walked in. From my perspective, this was positive rather than negative, but to William it was the end of the world.

As I listened to this saga of sin-related problems, something occurred to me. The roots of the girlfriend-related pain that William was processing had grown deep into all the other problems.

When she was "pulled up by the roots" out of his life, every other pain and problem from the past came up, too. Suddenly, brought to the surface was not just one weed but an entire weed patch replete with dirt, rocks and sticks. The complexity, the interconnected tentacles, the overwhelming workload required to clean up his whole life could possibly destroy William's fragile faith and, potentially, his life. He had already tried to commit suicide. To this new believer, one situation looked hopelessly interwoven with every other problem from the past and the present.

The devil incessantly tries, as one of his primary tactics, to convince us how hopelessly connected one problem is to the next. The web woven by the enemy has been designed to entrap us in deep despondency. However, things may not be as impossible as the devil wants us to believe—especially when we use the "divide and discern" principle.

The plan of the enemy must be revealed. As an example, he tries to make us think just because we struggle with a boss, our entire life is over. "Bad boss" does not have to equal "bad life." The entire future must not be forfeited because of a struggle in one area. Difficulties on the job should not be carried over to kids, cars and church. We must constantly counterbalance the negative with the positive. I would imagine the kids are alright, your spouse loves you, and your car still runs. I would guess most of you have a home to live in and someone to love you. When dealing with an ominous situation, we should not let one problem pervade our entire existence.

> When dealing with an ominous situation, we should not let one problem pervade our entire existence.

The book of Hebrews illustrates the "divide and discern" principle. The reason the Word of God is listed as living, powerful, and sharper than a double-edged sword is because it can divide and discern (see Hebrews 4:12).

Why is it important for the Word to be able to divide the soul from the spirit and the joints from the marrow? Why discern between the thoughts and the intent of the heart? Isn't Paul splitting unimportant theological hairs? Why such a particularized approach, such a detailed division? Isn't the Word of God powerful, alive, and sharp for better reasons than to divide and discern?

The author illustrates the depth of the diagnostic power of the Word of God. This gives us great advantage during spiritual conflict. At first the tangled, snarled web of interwoven problems and perplexing situations appears impossible to handle, but the Word of God—with the sharp edge of truth—has the power and precision to unravel the mess.

The Greek word Paul used for *sword* is not necessarily a long, battle-ready blade with a handle on one end, but a small scalpel-sized knife more closely resembling a surgical instrument. Properly applied principles of God's Word can divide each tentacle from the mass with the deftness of a doctor during surgery. Layer after tangled layer of sin or sickness can be removed; and with this tactic of the devil revealed, situations once hopeless can be handled in faith. Once removed from the complicated connection to the whole, each part, after being surgically separated, can be prayed over thoroughly and handled successfully. If the Word of the Lord can be specifically applied to a particular problem, our spiritual health is assured.

We can use the Word to divide into manageable parts what was once completely overwhelming. The Word divides layer after layer, then discerns the appropriate scriptural remedy. Apply the Word and watch it work. We can have success with the sword!

THE OFFENSIVE ABILITY OF THE WORD

A review of Ephesians 6 shows the protection provided by the spiritual armor. The soldier covers himself from head to toe with every protective piece of military apparel. As we have examined the different aspects of this apparel, we have noted the defensive posture of the soldier. We have analyzed each part and need to note that no other piece of armor has the flexibility and the mobility of the sword. When used correctly, it has the most offensive capabilities.

Inanimate objects are often subjugated by living organisms or human beings. In most cases, life triumphs over the lifeless and the cognizant over the mindless. The innate power of something or somebody living generally prevails, and that's why the possibility of a living sword seems interestingly implausible. However, remember Hebrews 4:12 declares the Word is alive. Because the Bible has an indescribable vitality through which it breathes and speaks, it is a living book. God's Word has energy. It moves, stirs and communicates with living man because it is alive.

The apostle Paul said all Scripture is inspired (see 2 Timothy 3:16). The word *inspiration* comes from the Greek word "theopneustos" which means "God-breathed." Little wonder why the Word of God is alive. It is "God-breathed."

The sword of the Spirit represents a living, breathing organism, not a clumsy, cumbersome organization. Scripturally, no other piece of armor has been listed as living; and this "alive" armor adds an offensive dimension needed to help us advance toward ultimate conquest!

Stephen, in Acts 7, describes the Scriptures as living oracles. They are not living just for the sake of being alive, but the Scriptures are alive to perpetuate a freedom-based life. The sword is not only to destroy the enemy but also should be used to cut chains of bondage and set captives free, because many prisoners of war wait for an aggressive, faith-filled soldier to rescue them. The liberating power of the Scriptures will be activated when a well-equipped soldier correctly applies the Word of God to a circumstance or situation. The book of Proverbs reminds us that the words of the Lord give life to those who find them. Let's give life and liberty to our loved ones by helping them find His Word. This will set them free.

THE SWORD IS ONLY AS GOOD AS THE SOLDIER

The Bible does us no good if we don't use it. How can the Scriptures benefit us if we never apply them? Paul instructed Timothy in the principle of using the Word wisely (see 2 Timothy 2:15).

You and I are the agents of our own spiritual success. This passage from the apostle Paul assures us that if we are responsible and diligent regarding our work in the kingdom of God, we can then use the Word of truth with accuracy. While enlisted in the Lord's army, we should strive to be the very best soldiers possible. Training in the Word qualifies us for spiritual success and victory in battle. The sword of the Lord really is only as good as the soldier who carries it.

The book of Psalms reveals a principle of protection regarding the Word. We are to hide the Word in our heart so in battle it can protect us (see Psalm 119:11).

The word *hidden* in this passage means "to protect." If we protect the Word in our hearts it will protect us during the heat of a spiritual battle. Again, the responsibility of victory is placed in my desire to protect the Word deep inside of my heart. I protect the Word, and it protects me. What an unbeatable combination!

The Message and Mantle: Success With the Sword

The "spirit of Jezebel" receives a lot of attention these days, maybe more than merited. This demonic spirit, named after an evil woman, was so named—not by the Bible—but by post-scriptural attempts to identify specific demonic activity. This is very admirable but possibly overstated. I feel if we base our names of spirits on what the Bible names as such, we will be on firm footing.

Jezebel represents a very evil influence over a very powerful man of God. The depth of the spiritual stupor she placed on Elijah is perplexing and worthy of study. But wisdom and accurate exegesis demands, even though somewhere along the way she got a demonic spirit named after her, we study the entire story (not just one character) and temper the trend to embellish evil above its relegated, subordinate position to our Savior.

Please consider this editorial interlude: Throughout this book, this chapter included, we have discussed spiritual warfare and how to defend and advance with a greater measure of success. For thematic harmony, let me unequivocally state my position. We are in a real spiritual war against a very formidable enemy. Wicked principalities and powers must be confronted now more than ever, and every spiritual soldier must be ready-minded, scripturally prepared and spiritually equipped.

It is imperative that we intercede against control, homosexually, witchcraft, confusion, depression, hopelessness and everything else (represented by Jezebel and other satanic influences) sent to destroy the church. We need distilled wisdom, accurate discernment, unflinching courage, and resolve like we've never had in order to survive and succeed. These comments on the "spirit of Jezebel" are not intended to contradict but complement the "armed and dangerous" emphasis of this book.

Because the satanic spirit that operated through Jezebel was around before her birth, it would be beneficial to enlarge our consideration to include the preexistence of the demonic activity that surrounded or influenced her. We need to generally consider Satan while we specifically consider Jezebel. Why were Satan and his army of fallen angels (demons) desperately trying to destroy the ministerial activities of Elijah? Could the decision to go after this great prophet be because of what he had done and some fear of what he could do? The key to understanding why, in the war room of the hideous underworld, the devil chose to draw a line in the spiritual sand, taking on the most powerful and productive prophet alive, is to understand the mission of this great man of God. Let's seriously look at Elijah and not just be preoccupied with Jezebel.

> We need distilled wisdom, accurate discernment, unflinching courage, and resolve like we've never had in order to survive and succeed.

In keeping with the theme of defending and advancing, Elijah represents battling for the present and building for the future. He destroyed the 450 prophets of Baal with a sword. The Ephesians 6 soldier reminds us, "the sword of the Spirit which is the Word of God" armor must be applied and activated. In 1 Kings we find Elijah doing just that. He shows how prophets (I don't think they were worthy of that title) of false gods can be slain by the weapon of the sword of the Spirit, the Word of God. This is battling for the present. But Elijah also illustrates building for the future with a word from an angel (messenger).

Elijah indicated his hopelessness by saying, "Things will always be as they have always been" (see 1 Kings 19:4). In his next assignment, he went in the strength of cake (bread) and water, because the journey was too great for him to attempt in his own power. To finally obliterate his enemy he would have to go in the strength from the messenger and transfer his prophetic mantle of anointing to Elisha, who represented the next generation. This is building for the future. The advance of kingdom expansion and apostolic authority into the next generation was, in this story, the bigger threat to the kingdom of darkness. Satan selected one of his most talented employees to accomplish this secret mission of destruction—namely Jezebel.

> The advance of kingdom expansion and apostolic authority into the next generation was, in this story, the bigger threat to the kingdom of darkness.

Because this story reflects the larger struggle between God and Satan, not just between Elijah and Jezebel, we should include in our thinking why Satan chose Jezebel to attack and destroy Elijah. I believe Satan did not want to face another generation of prophetically powerful leaders who would destroy his plan. He knew the next generation would propagate the work of Jehovah God with greater apostolic authority. He wanted to preempt the plan of God to pass the anointing from Elijah to Elisha. I think the devil saw Elisha coming up next and knew his best chance was to stop him before he got started.

It remains the same today. If Satan can cut off the channel of anointing and authority from one generation to the next, if he can make each family stop and start over through divorce, he will win. If he could succeed in breaking the blessing continuum in a local church through a split, he wins. If he can prevent a new believer from passing his or her faith on to the next generation, he will succeed. Thank God, the message (word from the messenger) will get us to the next generation. Even if people have to go through broom tree and cave experiences, every generation has a mandate to pass the mantle on to their successors. I hear the Lord saying to us, like He did to Elijah: "What are you doing here in this cave when I have called you to anoint Hazael, Jehu and Elisha?" If those who come behind us will judge us as faithful, it will be because we gave them what God gave us. The devil fears a godly generational connection more than we fight for one!

This story (1 Kings 19:5–17) reveals the reasoning behind the decision from Satan to choose Jezebel. But it also gives the church a four-step plan of attack against the devil and shows how to have victory over every evil influence sent to cut off our Elishas.

1. Wake up and get up (with angelic assistance) . . . get up and take the message.
2. Eat the bread (revelation) and drink the water (spirit) and it will sustain you all the way to the mount of God.
3. Hear the Word of God asking you, "What are you doing here?" (Remember, the Word of God is the sword of the Spirit.)
4. Pass on the mantle by anointing the next generation of spiritual headship.

Prayer and Armor Activation

After removing destructive seeds of false doctrine that had been sown into the fertile soil of a young church at Thessalonica, Paul again planted the seeds of truth. In a salutatory address to these believers, he suggested a defensive and offensive positional strategy. He said the Lord would guard them from the evil one. He also said the Lord would give the confidence needed to advance.

As we have been discussing, the armor protects us *from* something, but also *for* something. Putting on the armor of God does little good if we don't use it. We are not just called to be armed, but "armed and dangerous." Paul reveals how submitting a prayer request can augment this transition from defensive to offensive. He said, "Pray for us that the word of the Lord may run swiftly and be glorified, just as it is with you" (see 2 Thessalonians 3:1).

The power of prayer, as shown here, promotes rapid expansion and glorification of the Word of the Lord. Prayer helps activate the sword of the Spirit, which is the Word of God, until we can have confidence in the things we are doing and the things we will continue to do. The Amplified Bible reads:

> *Furthermore, brethren, do pray for us that the Word of the Lord may speed on (spread rapidly and run its course) and be glorified (extolled) and triumph, even as it had done with you. And we have confidence in the Lord concerning you, that you are doing and will continue to do the things which we suggest and with which we charge you.* —2 Thessalonians 3:1, 4

Wow! Advancing the kingdom—not just donning the armor. Now that's more like it!

The Bible refers to time with the use of two different original language words: *kairos* and *chronos*. The passing of calendar time or the recording of a religious activity such as prayer represents *chronos* time. However, when the Scriptures refer to the special dispensation of His "present-ness" as the fullness of time, this represents a set or proper time, a special season—a *kairos*.

Prayer can be the intersection of *kairos* time and *chronos* time. We must maintain a perfect balance between man's routine and God's restoration. We must remember that we serve a timeless God who dwells in eternity—a God who is not bound by time, space or matter. But in order for God to interact with His creation, He must interact with time. In order for us to fully interact with our Creator, we must pray.

John 5 tells us of a man who had been sick for a long time. The days and months gave way to years as the calendar pages kept turning (*chronos*); but at the appointed time (*kairos*), Jesus showed up to perform a miracle. At the perfect intersection of calendar time and a set season of divine timing, the man received his healing.

The spiritual significance of our prayers will become obvious when, in God's set season, a *kairos* intersects our *chronos*. It happened at the conception of Christ, when in the ordinary day-to-day routine of a teenage girl, the Holy Spirit overshadowed her with a divine appointment of *kairos* time. The same thing happened on the day of Pentecost when a regularly scheduled religious holiday turned into the birthday of the modern church.

I believe God will help us recover our passion in prayer when He invades our *chronos*. He wants to grant the prayers from our past by answering them with a "present-ness" of His set season. His predetermined purposes for our ministries will be actualized and His plan for our lives can be activated during *kairos*. Passion will return when we build, as well as battle, with great effectiveness.

Prayer: Battling and Building

Prayer can be offensive as well as defensive. Through prayer, you can gain new spiritual territory while defending territory previously obtained. Our spiritual success requires maintaining a balance of gaining (offensive) and guarding (defensive). This principle is illustrated in the life of Nehemiah.

Nehemiah had been given a mandate to rebuild the walls of Jerusalem, but when opposition from the enemy (Sanballat) came, he gave the people a strange military strategy: battle the enemy while you build the wall (see Nehemiah 4:17).

Most astonishingly, they built and battled very successfully. This massive undertaking was completed in fifty-two days. Interestingly, this text has numerous references to being prepared and protected for battle, yet we see no direct military engagement.

With all the talk of being prepared defensively, Nehemiah introduced a fresh, innovative spiritual offensive. What was his offensive tactic? Prayer! For Nehemiah, this prayer stayed the potential attack from the enemy.

After this initial prayer, the conspiracy continued with talk of an attack from the enemy. Once again Nehemiah took the offensive by praying (see Nehemiah 4:4–5).

Notice how he stayed on the offensive. His best defense was to continue offensively with prayer. Paul gives us another scriptural example of being protected in case of attack (see Philippians 4:6–7).

Are we ready to turn the table on our spiritual adversary, or are we preoccupied with protection? If we are passionate to the point of conquering new spiritual territory, we must not spend all of our time defending ground already gained. In short, we need help guarding so we can gain even more ground.

Paul gives us a profound suggestion. He understands no one can guard alone. Peace, which comes as the result of prayer, will help guard your heart.

If we get our guard up through prayer, we then will have a reserve of strength and energy for a new affront against the enemy. It may sound strange, but every spiritual soldier needs to stand guard over their heart using the peace of God. "The peace of God, which transcends all understanding, will guard your hearts and minds in Christ Jesus" (see Philippians 4:7 NIV)—that's how Paul encourages the saints in Philippi.

Peace of mind ensures a fresh passion for both spiritual and secular endeavors. This peace, activated by prayer, will release passion. Little prayer, little peace. No prayer, no peace. The peace that "guards while you gain" will bring emotional soundness. It will help resolve the unresolved and release the restrained. This emotional peace cuts deftly into any anxiety you may be dealing with. Every troubling and uneasy feeling of worry or doubt can be conquered. The anxiety issue is also handled by Paul within the context of Philippians, chapter four.

The King James rendering is very interesting. Verse six reads, "Be careful for nothing." This carefree, anxiety-free peace, which can only come through prayer, actually releases fear and restores a carefree attitude of faith.

When this balance of battling and building, gaining and guarding, is achieved, prayer becomes the defensive protection that covers your emotional heart but also frees you to move to more offensive strategies. This kind of peace penetrates deep, not with insufficient grace that would seem sacrilegious but with "sufficient grace" (see 2 Corinthians 12:9).

Obviously, from the context, we understand this does not refer to salvation grace, because herein the Lord directly answers a prayer for relief from constant satanic attack by reassuring the apostle Paul of sufficient grace. The Lord provided quantitative grace commensurate to the adversarial attack (thorn in the flesh).

The messenger from the enemy balanced Paul's possible personal exaltation by suggesting that if sufficient grace were withheld, Paul would not have had the peace to progress in ministry. He would have been on the defensive only. Through prayer, Paul is given grace and peace to stay on the offensive ministerially (see 2 Corinthians 12:8). The kingdom must be advanced through prevailing prayer and powerful, surpassing peace.

Prayer Principle #6:

Prayer Principle of Dividing and Discerning: Deals with Continuity

Use this prayer to untangle thoughts and feelings by dividing and discerning the power of God's Word. Unscramble confusing ideas and complicated situations by cutting, layer by layer, into the enemy's scheme. The sword of the Spirit, which is the Word of God, can prescribe a perfect remedy for every situation and give you a brand new paradigm.

Dear heavenly Father,

By faith, I take up the sword of the Spirit as part of my battle attire. Today I pick up the Word of God. The protection of Your spiritual armor is vital to my victory over sin. The battle is real, but with the right armor, I know I can prevail. I apply every principle as my protection.

You have not left me without defense against every evil aggression. Today, for the spiritual struggles that await me, I am equipped with the sword of the Lord. It is in my hand. It fits and feels good in my palm. I am ready, committed to the cause of Your kingdom, and confident in Your Word. Thank You, great God, that this sword is sharp, it is alive and it has power. It can cut decisively into the heart of any issue.

So, now I pray that the sword of the Lord helps me to take new spiritual ground—conquer new territory. With the Word, I move today into an offensive position. I activate the answer by prayer. Boldly and aggressively, I am on the move. Thoughts previously confusing and complicated are now unscrambled. With the sword, with the Word and through this prayer, my life is untangled.

Because this piece of my spiritual armor is activated, I can discern properly. I can divide layer by layer the circumstances surrounding my life.

Today I pray I can use the sword to cut the fetters of my friends and family. I know people who are in bondage. They are like prisoners of war, waiting to be released. Through this prayer, I war with the sword (the Word of God) until victory is won. Amen.

TWO POINT PRAYER PLAN:

1. START PRAYING NOW
2. NEVER STOP PRAYING

— CHAPTER EIGHT —

Walk the Warrior's Talk

Praying always with all prayer and supplication in the Spirit, being watchful to this end with all perseverance and supplication for all the saints.
—*Ephesians 6:18*

We have been discussing how prayer can be used to activate the soldier's armor according to Ephesians chapter six. When considering the protective military apparel in this passage, prayer could also be considered as a part of the armor. We must use the whole armor of God!

The picture painted by Paul provides us with a vivid image of a soldier dressed for battle. This warrior has his body covered and his hands full. He can hold or wear nothing more. Verse 18 lists prayer as a potentially powerful part of his protection and must not be overlooked as a non-armor option, but as a part of an essential spiritual outfit.

Prayer should become a part of our spiritual wherewithal by which we move into battle readiness and wholeness. Prayer provides protection (defense during an attack) and prayer promotes advancement and progress (offensive inspiration).

The Jewish New Testament Commentary by David Stern equates prayer to a part of the armor and weaponry provided by God. Stern says prayer is available as part of God's method to help us wage and win the war when struggling against unseen agents of darkness. The other-worldliness of prayer is the obvious key to spiritual success when engaging principalities, powers, and rulers of darkness. This battle won't be won with missiles and guns, but by prevailing prayer.

Even with all the aspects of prayer that can't be understood, the efficacy of prayer can be settled in our minds because when God lived a human life He prayed all the time. Everything else you can say about prayer pales in comparison to this truth. If God didn't think He could live a successful human life without prayer, I wonder why we think we can survive in this kingdom conflict without it.

As believers, we have been on the defensive long enough. Now it's time to conquer a new land and set up kingdom rule. It is not enough to defend ground we have previously conquered, or to merely maintain soil secured by someone else. We must defend, yet simultaneously conquer, new territory. The promise of possession given to the children of Israel in the book of Joshua exemplifies conquest as a part of our provision. God told them "Every place you take, I will give you" (see Joshua 1:3–5).

> It is not enough to defend ground we have previously conquered, or to merely maintain soil secured by someone else.

We must occupy offensively and then defend the new territory with the tenacity of a military minded occupation army. The mandate to occupy new spiritual lands demands that we launch a bold, dynamic prayer offensive. Conquering "Canaan" as a spiritual occupation exercise becomes possible when prayer activates our spiritual armor, energizes our hearts, and strengthens our mental tenacity. Don't be discouraged or become weary in well-doing, but remember the case of the children of Israel. Scripture reports God gave them the land little by little. But through effort and diligence, little by little can become a lot for us, just like it did for them.

Some defensive-minded spiritual soldiers use prayer like an emergency 911 call. The only time they call is when they are under spiritual attack and the enemy comes to conquer their faith, health, finances, or relationship. Offensive prayer remains as the single most important aspect when conquering your promised land. Don't wait until a spiritual crisis occurs or you're in jeopardy of losing territory; pray pro-actively to gain new ground now.

Guard Your Goal

Shifting to the offensive has been the theme throughout this book, and prayer makes possible this transition. New wisdom, powerful revelation, growth, maturity, ministry expansion, financial enhancement, territory enlargement, and armor activation all refer to moving into an offensive position spiritually. Progress, advancement and obtaining all that God has for us should be our goal. In verse 18 of Ephesians 6, notice how the word "all" was used three different times.

1. All prayer and supplication.
2. All perseverance and supplication.
3. For all the saints.

The "all" aspect of our prayers must be our objective so we can establish the kingdom of God in our lives. The "all" prayer is of utmost importance and must be our desired end. We must guard this goal (of the "all" prayer) much like a military watch is employed to protect troops and territory. Not to be redundant, but listen again to the language of verse 18:

Praying always with all prayer and supplication in the Spirit, being watchful to this end with all perseverance and supplication for all the saints.

Because prayer makes the offensive stance of the soldier possible, our goal of consistent prayer must be guarded. The word *watchful* in this verse means "not to sleep." The biblical prayer watch is one in which we guard ourselves from praying halfhearted prayers void of perseverance and supplications. These kinds of lukewarm prayers lend little offensive thrust and accomplish even less defensively. They conquer no enemies and hold onto no ground. Remember, we want to become *armed and dangerous* when waging war against the devil.

Spirit Supplication for the Saints

Perseverance, earnestness and determination in prayer are noble goals but, because of human weakness, mere determination will not sustain you. Sometimes only the Spirit can sustain you. During that season, the Spirit of God connects with the spirit of man and one prays "in the Spirit." A Spirit-led intercession ensures successful supplication.

When the Spirit prays in and through us, human limitations and weaknesses give way to intercession or "Spirit supplication." To pray "in the Spirit" means to consciously place ourselves under the influence of the Holy Spirit until the Spirit makes intercession for us. This cooperation and fellowship with the Spirit in prayer gives us the purpose of God for our prayers. Paul's instruction to the Romans strongly supports Spirit-inspired intercession (see Romans 8:26).

The word picture in this verse becomes remarkably vivid when we consult the original language. The phrase, *"The Spirit Himself makes intercession for us,"* comes from one Greek compound word, *sunantilambanomai,* which means "at the opposite end of," "helping carry the load." The Spirit gets on the opposite end of my prayer load and helps me. He doesn't carry the whole thing by Himself and I know it's too heavy for me alone. I'm glad God has promised to help me in my weakness. At that point, we co-labor in intercession so the heaviness is distributed between both parties . . . the Spirit and us.

Spirit-inspired prayer, alive with revelation and inspiration, may not look or sound like conventional prayer because human understanding and protocol do not control intercession. When spirit supplication takes place, divine earnestness and determination drive the prayer. A prayer warrior using spirit supplication can successfully wage war against the enemy.

Remember the two key principles of prayer we have been emphasizing at the end of each chapter:

1. Start praying now.
2. Never stop praying.

WALK THE WARRIOR'S TALK

In every military campaign the importance of a particular soldier, group of soldiers, or branch of service varies. A specialized unit may be called on for a "top secret" assignment and, at that point, become the most important unit in all of the military. In true kingdom conflict the most important special mission warrior that can be called on is a "prayer warrior." To a dedicated and confident soldier, talk is cheap. However, it seems some spiritual soldiers have put a premium on it.

In the natural, "talking it up" becomes a part of the pre-game plan. In the spiritual, a prayer warrior must resist the temptation of "talking it up" without walking out his/her prayer talk. That simply means pray, don't just talk about praying. Sadly, the church may be better at writing about prayer, preaching about prayer and singing about prayer than we are at praying. When we were growing up in church we were taught to pray until you "prayed through." I still think that is a good idea. Even discussions about prayer must be prayed-through. In these treacherous days, the Spirit of God seems to be inspiring prayer warriors to pray until they pray through, not just idly discuss prayer.

The term *prayer warrior* refers to a person who prays faithfully by employing powerful perseverance. A prayer warrior is the old-fashioned name for an intercessor. Both terms convey the same idea. However, I prefer the descriptive and insightful term *prayer warrior*. The picture we get from Paul illustrates vividly a warrior using prayer as a part of his strategy against the enemy (see 2 Timothy 2:3–5).

Because this passage could easily relate to a warrior of prayer, we can apply the principles taught in these verses to our prayer life. Paul instructs Timothy using metaphors of soldier, athlete, and farmer to enforce the concepts of endurance and perseverance. Paul told Timothy to be a prayer warrior.

Remember, perseverance in prayer is taught by Paul in Ephesians 6:18. Again the key principles of prayer are: start praying and then don't stop praying. Regardless of the situation or the circumstance, don't let the devil discourage you but, with faith, persevere until the answer arrives and the situation changes. Remember a "without ceasing" prayer set Peter free from his prison (see Acts 12:5). If the unrighteous judge yielded to the importunity prayer in Luke 11:8, why would we think that a righteous God won't.

> The plan of the enemy to entangle each one of us in the web of carnal business, dead-end deals and trivial matters can be foiled when we follow the Lord into the realm of apostolic authority.

As we study Paul's advice to Timothy, the second principle of prayer stands out: to disentangle yourself from the affairs of this life. It is difficult to be a real prayer warrior used in intercession yet be preoccupied with the mundane and temporal. The natural must give way to the supernatural. The plan of the enemy to entangle each one of us in the web of carnal business, dead-end deals and trivial matters can be foiled when we follow the Lord into the realm of apostolic authority.

The third prayer principle taken from Paul's counsel for Timothy is to follow spiritual orders. Notice how Paul speaks of pleasing the One who did the enlisting. The Captain of our Salvation knows the approach needed to succeed during spiritual conflict. Because His ways are not ours, we must please Him by following directives and assignments. The best way to defeat the devil and ensure victory is to follow the scriptural code of conduct during spiritual conflict. The sign of a mature, military-minded prayer warrior is surrendering one's own desires, aspirations, and control to the Lord of Hosts. We must trust His discretion and direction.

Let's review the rules of competing in victorious prayer according to 2 Timothy 2:5:

1. Don't quit . . . persevere and endure.
2. Don't get tangled up with the temporal; disentangle with the temporal transactions to engage the eternal.
3. Trust the direction of the leader. Follow because of faith.

ONGOING INCENSE

"Every word you have ever spoken is still out there somewhere—alive," said Mrs. Bower, my high school Spanish teacher. "Words never die," she continued, "so choose your words carefully, because they may eventually return to you—for you to swallow." Looking back, I think she was onto something seriously spiritual, and I think she knew it.

Scientifically speaking, sound travels through airwaves on an infinite line. Spiritually speaking, this principle is true not only for idle words of conversation but also for specific words spoken in prayer. Prayers live forever . . . just consider the possibilities of that. Think of every prayer ever uttered remaining alive and powerful, still effective and able to create. Can you imagine a prayer warrior's "war cry" continuing until the enemy is defeated and the victory is won—even after they're gone?

Argue the theological fine points, if you like. Try to determine the final destination of answered prayers, if you wish. But don't discount this: when we pray, He will answer. He hears me the first time I pray, so, even if an answer has been delayed, that request is still alive. John saw into the activities of heaven and watched as the elders bowed down before the Lamb of God with a bowl full of prayers of the saints that were still making fragrant incense—ongoing incense. I like the sound (and smell) of that. It is difficult to establish when and how prayers produce incense, but of this one thing I'm sure: experience outweighs debate and discussion. When a prayer warrior establishes facts out in the field of prayer through experience, that tends to settle the debate. Such was the case of the "war cries" of one Indianapolis, Indiana, saint.

She died with her family still lost but, for this warrior of prayer, her hope of answered prayer lived on. They called her Grandma French and she faithfully labored in the trenches of intercession for who knows how long. The generation who knew her personally is almost gone from our home church, but her story remains.

To the unbelieving, every prayer request from her for family served more as a reminder of what God hadn't done as compared to what He could do. It had been so long with so little result. To a weaker warrior, each prayer prayed could have been more of a haunting indication of unanswered prayer than a celebration of the possibilities of prayer. But Grandma French didn't have much time for debate or discussion. She was too busy praying and interceding for her lost loved ones. When she went to her grave without the encouragement of answered prayer, it appeared as if this prayer warrior lost the battle. But time would reveal she would win the war. Within one year of her passing, 30 of her children, grandchildren and great-grandchildren came to saving faith and became involved in church and ministry. She died, but her prayers remained alive and effective until they accomplished their intended purpose.

I think Grandma French exemplifies the warrior of prayer found in Ephesians 6. She followed the admonition mentioned therein. With the focus of a military mandate, she truly walked out the warrior's talk. I believe we can find strength from her example and encouragement from this passage to watch over our request with perseverance.

"Praying always with all prayer and supplication in the Spirit, being watchful to this end with all perseverance and supplication for all the saints."

PRAYER AND PRISONERS

Of the 17 chapters in the book of Acts making reference to prayer, two are found in settings containing soldiers. Let's look at Acts 12 and Acts 16. Both of these scriptural examples indicate how an enemy soldier cannot prevail against powerful prayer warriors who have activated their spiritual armor.

In Acts 12, political opposition results in the first apostle martyred—James was murdered. Also, Peter was placed in prison to await his execution. Sixteen soldiers, body chains, and iron gates could not stop the impact of the warriors of prayer. Political oppression cannot control an angel sent on assignment because of prayer.

In Acts 16, Paul and Silas were thrown into prison for casting out a spirit of soothsaying from a woman. After being beaten, they were bound by stocks in the inner part of the prison. However, at midnight these preachers in prison began to pray and praise the Lord, not according to the facts but according to their faith. These prayers (and praises) released an earthquake that loosed their bonds and set them free.

The freedom of these faithful warriors frightened the guard until he was bound by fear. When prayer activates our spiritual armor, the roles are reversed on the enemy. We can move from the defensive to the offensive by being set free from the bondage of Satan and, in turn, binding him in the name of Jesus and through the power of prayer. This one principle can revolutionize your prayer life and energize your entire existence.

Activating the divine armor and standing firm in the battle requires a life of dependence on God in prayer. We must pray at all times but, for continued spiritual success, we need faith accompanied with action. We should believe something strongly enough to act on what we believe. This offensive approach keeps us from being overcome by fatigue, fear, and discouragement. Remember, this is not neutral territory but a war zone where we must fight to a conclusion. By the word already given, let us wage a good warfare with faith and a good conscience (see 1 Timothy 1:18–19). I believe the six prayer strategies discussed in this book will enable you to become *armed and dangerous*.

Going In and Going All Out

The first meeting between Vice President Richard Nixon and Winston Churchill involved a routine diplomatic assignment for the vice president. Nixon greeted the great military man at Andrews Air Force Base and escorted him back to the White House. In order to make conversation with the renowned World War II hero, Nixon turned the topic to the French invasion of Indochina. After listening to Nixon's comments, Churchill offered his opinion, "They made a decision to go in but not to go all out." Many believe the same assessment may be valid regarding the United States' involvement in Vietnam. Most believe if the allied forces had gone "all out" in Vietnam, victory would have been guaranteed. In both cases, the armies may have been armed but not dangerous.

> They made a decision to go in but not to go all out.

If our only intention is becoming armed, the armor applied according to Ephesians 6 may be adequate. But if we want to go "all out," we must activate the armor through prayer and become a dangerous threat to the evil principalities and powers. Let's go "all out" for the cause of the kingdom!

To become *armed and dangerous* requires that we apply and activate our armor through prayer. In our efforts to move us from *armed but not dangerous* to *armed and dangerous,* prayer remains the missing element. Remember, the Ephesians 6 soldier did not need more armor; he just needed to activate the armor issued.

To be dangerous to the devil is the desired objective of Paul's instructions to the Ephesians. He knew wrestling against an enemy of this magnitude must include the armor applied in Ephesians 6:12–17, but also activated by the prayer of verse 18. Prayer, as a vital part of our spiritual armor and as an activating ingredient to the other five pieces, enables us to become not just *armed* but *armed and dangerous.* Certainly Paul intended to equip the Christian soldiers with armor and empower them with prayer.

EPILOGUE

SUMMARY OF THE SIX PRAYER PRINCIPLES

The Bible brings tremendous benefits to us: education, revelation and inspiration, not to mention salvation. We face the challenge of turning the benefits of the Bible into application. It is difficult to take the lessons from the page and apply them to our personal life. While application is important, activation is imperative. To apply the passage without activating the principle is like having faith without works. (Remember: *Faith without works is dead.* James 1:6.) Application starts with the head and heart, but activation uses the hands, mouth, and feet. A*pply* means to "put it on"—like a mother applies medicine to a child's cut—and *activate* means "turn it on"—like activating an engine by turning the key. Put on the armor . . . turn on the soldier. Prayer helps turn the application into activation. Faith-filled prayer activates your spiritual armor. While application may be easily identified by your head and heart, it must be activated through hands, mouth, and feet.

The passage found in Ephesians 6 is an example of application needing activation. There we find a detailed description of a soldier replete with armor to wear and an enemy to fight. But how do we fight against an unseen enemy?

We have learned how to apply and activate each piece of armor with a specific prayer strategy. Each of the six prayer strategies is intended to apply and activate a particular piece of armor. Let me briefly review the six prayer principles associated with a piece of armor.

Remember: each prayer principle has an application prayer associated with it. These are found at the end of each chapter.

Prayer Principle #1:

Prayer Principle of Maturity: Deals With Selfishness

The belt of truth is the protective prayer over the ability to spiritually reproduce. Pray this prayer in order to transition into a mature Christian—ready to surrender to God's plan of spiritual reproduction.

Prayer Principle #2:

Prayer Principle of Passion: Deals With Self-Righteousness

The breastplate of righteousness is the covering for the vital organs, particularly the heart. The heart speaks of passion. This prayer will help you discern the *kairos* timing of God's set season and revitalize your zeal for the kingdom.

Prayer Principle #3:

Prayer Principle of Right Timing: Deals With Confusion

Sandals are for footing, foundation and direction. When this part of the armor is applied and activated through prayer, proper alignment in the government of God will bring peace, progress, and increase.

Prayer Principle #4:

Prayer Principle of Persuasion: Deals with the Opportunistic Enemy

The shield of faith represents the protection from the darts of the devil. This protection comes by becoming a doer and not just a hearer of the Word. You can use faith for defending yourself while simultaneously attacking the enemy. Faith is persuasion, and persuasion inspires action. This prayer restores your faith and inspires action by destroying discouragement.

Prayer Principle #5:

Prayer Principle of Focus:
Deals with Double-mindedness

The helmet prayer secures proper approach to thinking, reasoning and revelation. The prayer for proper thinking is a simple one that releases God's wisdom and rebukes the devil's lies. This prayer for single-mindedness protects our spiritual nerve center. The devil uses double-mindedness because it brings instability at every level. This prayer approach will encourage stable saints with stable spirits.

Prayer Principle #6:

Principle of Dividing and Discerning:
Deals with Continuity

Use this prayer to untangle thoughts and feelings by dividing and discerning the power of God's Word. Unscramble confusing ideas and complicated situations by cutting, layer by layer, into the enemy's system and scheme. The sword of the Spirit, which is the Word of God, can prescribe a perfect remedy for every situation and give you a brand new paradigm.